EVERY CHILD'S
BOOK OF
MUSIC
AND
MUSICIANS

SHULA DONIACH

Burke Books  LONDON & TORONTO

The author thanks a number of her friends and colleagues, especially Felix Aprahamian and Yekutiel Shur, for valuable comments and suggestions; also Reginald Tristram, her husband, for collaborating in the preparation of this book; and Edmond Kapp, for permission to reproduce his drawing: *Discovering Music*.

The author and the publishers thank F. T. Holmes for supplying twelve original drawings for this book; also the following for permission to reproduce illustrations and quotations from modern works of which they hold the copyright:
The Amadeus Quartet; BBC Pictorial Publicity; Boosey & Hawkes Ltd.; Breitkopf & Härtel; British & Continental Music Agencies; The Trustees of the British Museum; J. & W. Chester Ltd.; J. Curwen & Sons Ltd.; Decca Record Co. Ltd.; Ernest Read Music Association; Harold Holt Ltd.; London Philharmonic Orchestra Ltd.; Miss Elisabeth Lutyens; Godfrey MacDomnic; Mirrorpic; The Museum of Modern Art, New York; Novello & Co. Ltd.; Miss Daphne Oram; Oxford University Press; Press Association; Radio Times Hulton Picture Library; *Reynolds News;* Royal Opera House, Covent Garden; Schott & Co. Ltd.; Spring Books Ltd.; *The Sunday Times;* United Music Publishers Ltd.; Universal Edition (Alfred A. Kalmus) Ltd.; Universal Edition (London) Ltd.; Joseph Williams Ltd.

ISBN 0 222 00178 x

Burke Publishing Company Ltd.,
14 John Street, London, WC1N 2EJ.
Burke Publishing (Canada) Ltd.,
P.O. Box 48, Toronto-Dominion Centre,
Toronto 111, Ontario.
Printed in Great Britain
by T. and A. Constable Ltd., Edinburgh

EVERY CHILD'S
BOOK OF
MUSIC
AND
MUSICIANS

Contents

Discovering music

CHAPTER ONE

What is Music?

MUSIC IN NATURE · MAN-MADE MUSIC · MATERIALS
OF MUSIC · MUSIC AND THE OTHER ARTS · MUSIC, A
WORLD OF ITS OWN

Any sounds that we listen to and enjoy might be called music. In this sense, Nature is full of music. There is the music of the wind in the trees, of waves breaking on the sea-shore, of water rippling in the brook or rushing in the river. All these are fascinating sounds that we never tire of listening to. Even more interesting are the songs of the birds, for birds are live creatures expressing themselves. What do they say? We can only guess, while we marvel at the beauty of some of their calls, at the way they some-times repeat quite complicated tunes and sometimes vary them in unex-pected ways, so that we can never be quite sure what they are going to sing next.

Bird-song is the nearest thing in Nature to human song. When man makes music he, too, can sing beauti-ful tunes, often repeating and varying them, just as the birds do. But there is something more in human music, for besides wanting to express his feelings,

man has a strong impulse to build up his tunes into satisfying or exciting shapes. Think of any song you know and sing it in your head (or aloud, if you prefer); you will find that it is made up of a number of short tunes. Sometimes these tunes are repeated, sometimes they are varied, but always they follow one another in such a way as to form a definite whole. The art of making tunes and building them up into definite shapes is called *com-position*.

Besides being able to produce musical sounds with his voice, man also has any number of other sounds to choose from for his music-making, because he can invent musical instru-ments and play on them. There are percussion instruments, like the drum; wind instruments, like the recorder; plucking instruments, like the guitar; keyboard instruments, like the piano; and many, many others, each having its own special sound or tone-colour.

You too can invent tunes, compose

songs, and play instruments. Perhaps you do already. Perhaps you are reading this book because you like music and want to know more about it. Some of the essential things in music are so simple that you can find them in any song you know. For instance, sing a cheerful marching song, marching round the room while you sing. Notice the regular sounds your feet make as you march: *"one, two; one, two"*. This regular pattern in the music is called *rhythm*. Now sit down and sing the same song again, listening to yourself and noticing how your voice goes up and down. What you are noticing now is called *pitch*.

All the music in the world has

"O hush thee, my baby"

rhythm and pitch, like the song you have just been singing. Usually the rhythm is regular, so that you can march or dance to it, if you want to; and the pitch is usually clear, so that you can find the tune and sing it in your head. You can try this out by listening to any music on the radio.

The mood of a piece of music depends very much on its speed, or *tempo*, as it is called in music. For instance, mothers usually sing their children to sleep in a rather slow tempo, so as to have a soothing effect. Think of any lullaby you know, and try singing it in a fast tempo. Do you think that would help a baby to go to sleep?

Musical sounds vary from the softest whisper of violins to the loudest thunder of drums. This quality of loudness or softness is known as *dynamics;* the drowsy feeling of a lullaby would depend on its dynamics as well as on its tempo. Imagine a mother singing her lullaby in the right tempo, but with the wrong dynamics—that is, slowly enough, but loudly instead of softly. What will the baby do then, poor thing? Don't you think it will wake up and cry?

Now imagine the mother singing her lullaby in the right tempo and with the right dynamics—that is, slowly and softly, but *without the words.* (Try humming it yourself.) Here at last is the soothing, drowsy mood— just what the baby needs, even without the words, and it will be asleep in no time.

To take another example: what will happen to you if you sing your marching song in the right tempo—that is, at walking speed—but with the wrong dynamics — that is, very softly? Won't you find yourself creeping along on tiptoe? Now sing your marching song in the right tempo and with the right dynamics, but without the words, still marching round the room while you sing. How does it feel? Not bad, is it? In fact, you can march to it just as well without words as with them.

Do you see how music is like poetry? It has different kinds of moods and it is arranged in patterns. At the same time it is different from poetry, because it doesn't always use words; it can express feelings in pure sound.

Music is also like painting, because it can suggest a picture. Look at this picture of *The Submerged Cathedral*. You can see that it is a great cathedral sunk in the depths of the sea. There is a piece of music for the piano called *The Submerged Cathedral,* by Debussy, which suggests a similar picture. Try to hear a record of it; or perhaps you can get someone to play it to you. Hear how the music suggests deep water, then something gigantic rising from the depths, then the clang of great bells, as if the cathedral had come to the surface. Slowly

and sadly it sinks back again — until finally you hear the muffled sound of far-off bells under rippling water, dying away into the depths.

Music can tell a story too. Have you ever heard a piece of music for orchestra by Paul Dukas, called *The Sorcerer's Apprentice*? If not, do try to borrow a record of it. The music follows the story so clearly that you can hear just what is happening at each stage of it: the sorcerer leaving, the lazy apprentice trying a magic spell on the broom, the broom fetching water from the river, faster and faster, the apprentice trying to stop it, more and more water; the apprentice, unable to stop the broom, breaks it in

9

two; silence; then each half of the broom fetching more and more water, faster, faster, the place is flooded, the water is rising and rising; at last the sorcerer is back; the magic spell; all is peaceful as before. But cleverly as the music suggests the story, it even more cleverly makes us feel how frightened the apprentice is at the disaster, and how grateful he is when his master has put everything right again. We can almost hear him saying, at the very end: "*Dear* master, *please* forgive me. I will *never* do such a thing again!"

Of all the arts, perhaps it is dancing that is closest to music. In fact, we can hardly think of dancing without music. Quite a number of pieces that we hear at concerts were originally composed for dancing—for example, *Swan Lake* (by Tchaikovsky) and *The Firebird* (by Stravinsky). Sometimes

the music itself is so beautiful that we can enjoy it just as much without the dancing. But in music of this kind there is always a strong element of dancing—something in the rhythm that sets us dancing inside ourselves.

Do you see how music joins hands with the other arts? Sometimes it even links them together, for music that suggests a picture can also tell a story, and music that tells a story can also express feelings and invite us to share them. Music can borrow the moods and shapes of poetry, as it does in songs, or the lilting patterns of dancing, as it does in dances. At the same time it can stand perfectly well alone, for music is a magical gateway to another world—a world of sound, with its own shapes and colours and lilting patterns, its own feelings and adventures. This is the world we are going to explore.

LISTEN TO THESE RECORDS

Debussy: The Submerged Cathedral. *Dukas:* The Sorcerer's Apprentice.

CHAPTER TWO

A World of Sound

MORE ABOUT RHYTHM: PULSE, ACCENT, RHYTHMIC
PATTERNS · PHRASES AND CADENCES · MORE ABOUT
PITCH: SCALES, TONALITY · MELODY AND HARMONY ·
TIMBRE: VOICES, HARMONICS, INSTRUMENTS

THE FIRST THING to do in a world of sound is to listen.

What shall we listen for first? Let us find out some more about rhythm. If you listen to almost any piece of music, on a record or on the radio, you will find that there is a regular throb going on behind it all the time which you can pick out and tap or clap. This regular throb is called *pulse* or *beat*. Listen for a little while, quietly tapping the pulses. If the music is in a fast tempo, the pulses will be fast, and if the music is in a slow tempo, the pulses will be slow. Now sing any song you know, at the same time tapping the regular pulse, and noticing if it is fast or slow. For instance, *D'ye ken John Peel?* has a quick beat, and *God save the Queen* has a rather slow one.

We have already noticed that there is something in a marching song that sets us marching. This is partly its regular pulse, but it is also the lively *"one,* two; *one,* two" of its rhythm.

Do you know how to beat time to a march? Start with both hands up; bring them down smartly on *"one",* then raise them on "two". We call this "two-time". Some marches are in "four-time": *"one,* two, three, four; *one,* two, three, four." You can beat four-time like this: *"Down,* in, out, up; *down,* in, out, up." (Or, if you prefer, you can beat time with the right hand only: *"down,* left, right, up.")

Down,   in,   out,   up

Hum, sing or whistle a tune and try to beat time to it. It might be in two-

11

time or four-time. Or it might possibly be in three-time: *"one,* two, three." If it is in three-time, you can beat *"down,* out, up; *down,* out, up." (Or, with the right hand only: *"down,* right, up.")

You have probably seen conductors of choirs or orchestras waving their arms about. Their movements are based on the ones you have just been making yourself, in two-time, three-time or four-time, depending on the kind of music being played or sung. This is how conductors keep singers or players in time together.

The regular emphasis of the first beat of each group of two, three or four beats is called *accent.* Conductors show this regular accent by their *"down"* beat.

The next thing to notice about rhythm is that every tune has its own *rhythmic pattern.* Sing *Charlie is my darling,* or any other song you know, at the same time clapping or tapping the tune as you sing. Be sure you are clapping the actual sounds of the tune, and not just the regular pulse behind it. Now sing it again, still clapping or tapping the tune, but singing without the words, just to "lah". Now clap the tune again, but without singing at all. What you have just been clapping is the rhythmic pattern. Try clapping this to someone who knows the tune and see if they can recognise it. Also when you listen to the radio, try to follow the

rhythmic patterns in the music and clap or tap them as you listen.

The next thing to listen for is the shape of the music. As we found out in the first chapter, all songs consist of a number of short tunes, building up to a complete whole. Each of these short tunes is called a *phrase.* The phrases very often correspond to the rhythmic pattern—for example, *Glory, glory, alleluia.* Some phrases begin on a down-beat, like the first phrase of *Early one morning;* and some begin on an up-beat, like *D'ye ken John Peel?* Sometimes there is time for a breath between one phrase and the next, as there is in *Glory, glory, alleluia;* and sometimes there is not, as in *Early one morning.*

Glo - ry, Glo - ry, Al - le lu - - ia - *(breath)*
Glo - ry, Glo - ry, Al - le lu - - ia - *(breath)*
Ear - ly one morn - ing just as the sun was ri - sing
(straight on with no pause for breath)
I heard a maid sing - ing in the val - ley below.

Phrases are the building-blocks of music. Like building-blocks, they are often arranged in pairs, one phrase asking to be balanced by another. In most folk-songs either the first phrase is simply repeated, as in *All through the night,* or else the first phrase is answered by a second slightly different one, as in *Charlie is my darling.* Or the same rhythmic pattern is used for the balancing phrase with different pitch, as in *Glory, glory, alleluia.* This first pair of phrases is usually balanced by another pair, making four phrases in all.

When a tune comes to a definite end, the ending is called a *cadence*, as at the word "below" in *Early one morning,* or at the word "morning" in *D'ye ken John Peel?*

A good conductor, as well as keeping everybody in time, helps us to hear the shape of the music. He helps us to hear the beginnings of phrases and makes us feel how the phrases move on towards a cadence. He does this by showing the performers where to pause (or breathe), and by altering the tempo and dynamics so as to make us feel all the excitement of moving on towards a goal, or building up to a climax.

When you listen to music, what do you notice about the pitch? It goes up and it goes down, and you can often follow the tune and sing it in your head. Many tunes are quite easy to follow because they make sense. You can hear that the sounds belong together, in much the same way as words do in a sentence. This is because they are all related to one central note, the home note. Most tunes end on the home note, so it is easy to find and sing.

To get some idea how sounds of different pitch can belong together, try this at the piano: press down the first of any group of three black keys to make a sound (figure 1), then the one next to it, and the next; then the

next group of two black keys, one after the other, so that you have played five sounds in succession; then play all these sounds back again, so that you end up where you started. Now do the whole thing again. Can you hear how all these sounds seem to belong together like a family? These families of sounds are called *scales*. And, like families, each scale has a character of its own.

Now play a scale all on white keys. Try the one that begins on D (figure 1), eight notes up and eight notes down again, like this: D E F G A B C D; D C B A G F E D. Don't you think it has a somewhat peculiar flavour? Some sea shanties are made up from this set of sounds, and it makes them rather attractive; for example, *What shall we do with a drunken sailor?* begins like this:

Words:
What shall we do with a drunken sailor?
Rhythmic pattern:
Tum tid - dy tum tid - dy tum ta - ra - ra
Names of notes:
 A   A   A   A   A   A   A   D   F A
Beat:
One   two   three four One two three four

It ends like this:

Words:
Ear - ly   in   the morn   -   ing
Rhythmic pattern:
Rum tum tum tum ta   -   ra
Names of notes:
 C   A   G   E   D   D
Beat:
One two three four *One* two   three four

Now play the scale of eight notes that starts on C (figure 1) all on white keys: C D E F G A B C; C B A G F E D C. It sounds familiar, doesn't

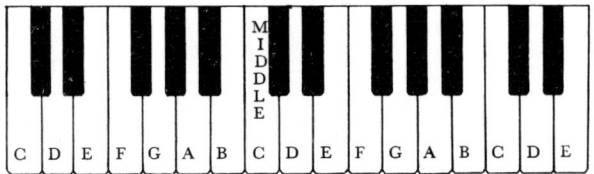

FIGURE 1

it? Many of the songs we sing and hear are made up from this set of sounds, which is called the *major* scale. See if you can play *God save the Queen,* starting on C and using one finger. You will find that you can play it quite correctly without using any black keys. Now try to play it in the scale of G major, that is, starting it on G. You will find that in order to get the fourth note right you will have to use the black key between F and G; this is called F sharp. Now play a scale of eight notes starting on G, up and down, but, instead of F, play F sharp: G A B C D E F sharp G; G F sharp E D C B A G.

If you try to pick out a major scale starting on F and using white keys only, you will find that the B sounds wrong. Instead of the B, play the black key between A and B; this is called B flat: F G A B flat C D E F; F E D C B flat A G F. Now you have played the scale of F major.

In a similar way you can find a major scale starting anywhere on the piano. Your ear will tell you where to use the black keys.

Another scale that is very familiar is the *minor* scale. You can get a fairly good idea of this by playing the scale all on white keys that starts on A (figure 1), like this: A B C D E F G A; A G F E D C B A. Or you might try this version of it: A B C D E F G sharp A; A G sharp F E D C B A. Don't you think it has a rather sad effect, compared with the cheerful major scale? A good many sad songs are made up from the sounds of the minor scale—for instance, *The oak and the ash.* If you like, you can try to pick out minor scales starting on D or E or any other note. Here, again, your ear will tell you where to use black keys.

Some songs begin on the first note of the scale, which is called the *tonic,* for instance, *God save the Queen.*

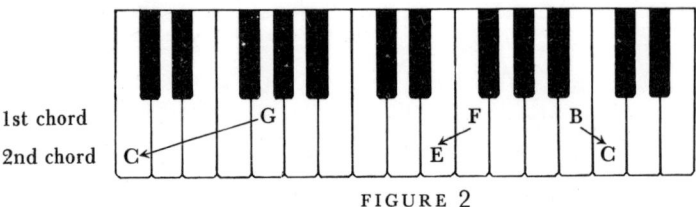

1st chord
2nd chord

FIGURE 2

14

Some songs begin on the fifth note of the scale, which is called the *dominant,* for instance, *Glory, glory, alleluia.* Some begin on the third note of the scale, which is called the *mediant,* for instance, *D'ye ken John Peel?* Most songs end on the tonic, and that is why it is sometimes called the home note.

The next time you hear some music, whether it is at a concert or on a record or on the radio, you can notice whether it is cheerful or sad, and whether it sounds as if it uses the notes of the major or minor scale, or whether it sounds slightly peculiar, in which case it probably uses a scale of its own. Try to pick out the tune and sing it in your head while listening, and notice how it moves on to its home note, or tonic.

Mark the note that rises,
  Mark the notes that fall;
Mark the time when broken,
  And the swing of it all.

So when night is come
  And you have gone to bed,
All the songs you love to sing
  Shall echo in your head.

R. L. Stevenson.

When you sing a song without the words, you are singing its *melody.* In the world of sound there are many songs without words—many melodies all built up of a number of phrases. A melody can be sung or played by itself, but it sounds a good deal richer if it is combined with other melodies, as it is in part-songs, or if it has an accompaniment, either on the piano or other instruments. If a melody is being sung or played by itself, you hear only one sound at a time, but if there is an accompaniment or if it is combined with other melodies, you can hear two or more sounds going on at the same time. The art of arranging sounds to be played or sung at the same time is called *harmony.*

Let us see if we can find out something about harmony at the piano. Play middle C with the thumb of your right hand and hold it down; then play E with your middle finger and hold that down too; now play G with your little finger and hold that down as well (figure 1). Listen for a moment . . . Let go and then play all three notes at once, like this: $\begin{smallmatrix} G \\ E \\ C \end{smallmatrix}$ Hold them down and listen. Now you have played a *chord.* How does it sound? Rich and satisfying? Now play the same chord again, but adding the C below with the left hand. Better still? The sounds seem to blend smoothly together. This kind of chord is called a *concord.*

Now play any four notes on white keys next door to each other, first one after the other, then all four at once. Now you have played another chord. But this one is quite different from the first one. The sounds seem to be clashing with one another. This kind of chord is called a *discord*. In fact, any chord of two or more tones which sound as if they are clashing is a discord, and any chord of two or more tones which sound smooth and satisfying is a concord.

Discords often seem to be asking to be followed by a concord. For instance, play E with the left thumb and the F next to it with the right thumb, both together. Listen. Is this a discord or a concord? Yes, of course, a discord. Now with the left index finger play the black key next to the E, and with the right index finger play the black key next to the F, both together. Listen. Is this a discord or a concord? Yes, a concord. Now play them again, the discord followed by the concord, and notice how the discord seems to be answered by the concord.

Let us try another pair of chords. With the right hand play $\frac{B}{F}$ together, followed by $\frac{C}{E}$. Play this pair of chords several times, noticing how the $\frac{C}{E}$ chord seems to complete the $\frac{B}{F}$ chord. Do you think a song or piece could end on the $\frac{B}{F}$ chord? No; it sounds unfinished, as if it were asking to go on, but when you follow it by the $\frac{C}{E}$ chord

it sounds complete. This pair of chords, where the second completes the first, is called a *resolution*. It could be used to accompany the end of some melodies, but if you want it to sound really final, play it again, adding these notes with the left hand: G with the first chord and C with the second as shown in figure 2. Now you have played a *perfect cadence*. You could use it to finish up any number of songs with: *Early one morning, Glory, glory, alleluia,* and many others.

Try to find some more concords and discords on the piano. Also try to hear the perfect cadences in the music you listen to. You will find that a great many pieces end with a perfect cadence.

A chord of two notes can also be called an *interval*. Play F and B together; then, calling F the first note, count up to B; which you will find is the fourth note. The interval $\frac{B}{F}$ is called a *fourth*. Now play E and C together, and count this interval, calling E the first and counting up to C. You will find that this interval is a *sixth*. (So you see that in figure 2 you played a fourth followed by a sixth.)

Some chords of three notes are called *triads*. For example, the chord $\begin{smallmatrix} G \\ E \\ C \end{smallmatrix}$ which you played on p. 15 is a triad. It is made up of the two intervals $\frac{E}{C}$ and $\frac{G}{E}$. Can you work out what kind of intervals they are? Yes, each of

16

them is a *third*. And as this triad is built up on the tonic of C major, it is called the tonic triad of C major, or, more simply, the C major triad.

Try to find some more major triads on the piano. You can do it like this: play the first five notes of any major scale (say F major) one after the other; now pick out the first, the third and the fifth (the tonic, the mediant and the dominant; or, if you know tonic sol-fa, "doh-me-soh"), and play them together.

In the same way, you could find some minor triads. Play the first five notes of any minor scale (say A minor) one after the other; then pick out the first, the third and the fifth and play them together. This is a minor triad. Can you hear how different it sounds from the bright major triad?

Try playing triads all on white keys. Can you tell by the sound if they are major or minor?

Chords are useful for accompanying melodies, especially if you fit the chord to the melody note by making sure that your chord includes that note. For instance, play or sing *Early one morning* in C major. It starts on C, so find a chord that includes C: the best one is the C major triad, because the first phrase of this song includes all its notes, C, E and G. In fact, we could call this a chord tune. It is quite helpful to notice that some tunes are chord tunes and some tunes are scale tunes. Here are some scale tunes: *Charlie is my darling, Wraggle-taggle gipsies, Bluebells of Scotland*. And here are some chord tunes: *Early one morning, What shall we do with a drunken sailor?, The Ash Grove*. And, of course, there are many which are a mixture of scale tunes and chord tunes—for example, *Glory, glory, alleluia* and the end of *Early one morning*.

Listen to some music and try to notice when the tunes are chord tunes, when they are scale tunes, and when they are mixed, and how the chords fit in.

Another thing to listen for in the world of sound is tone colour, which is here called *timbre* (a French word, pronounced "tambr"). Every voice, every instrument, has a special colour or timbre of its own. You can usually tell at once if a song is being sung by a man or a woman. The difference of timbre here is mainly due to difference of pitch. Have you ever heard a tape-recorder playing a singing voice at the wrong speed? If it is a man's voice and is played twice as fast as it should be played, it sounds just like a woman's voice. And if a woman's voice is played twice as slow as it should be played, it sounds just like a man's voice. This is because pitch depends on the frequency of vibrations which reach your ear as sounds. If they are faster (that is, more vibrations per second), the sound will be higher; if they are slower (that is,

17

fewer vibrations per second), the sound will be lower.

The timbre of a sound depends on a number of other things besides pitch; it depends largely on the way it is produced; whether it comes from an instrument that is being blown or scraped, beaten or plucked. Secondly, it depends on whether the sound is pure or mixed — just as you can have pure or mixed colours in painting. For instance, just as you can have a red colour in a picture with traces of yellow in it, so you can have the sound of C in a piece of music with traces of E in it — and traces of other notes too.

Try this experiment at the piano: press the right pedal down with your foot and hold it down. Now put the first finger of your left hand over the lowest C on the piano, and the first finger of your right hand over the next C above that. Play them both together as loudly as you can, keeping your foot down. Now listen for about half a minute and you will gradually hear several other sounds humming very faintly, besides the two loud C's. The G, C and E in the middle of the piano are vibrating in sympathy with the two low C's, and it is this mixture of sounds which gives the piano tone its rich colour or timbre.

If this does not work very well on your piano, you can check the experiment by another one like this: press down middle C with the middle fin-ger of your right hand very gently, without letting it sound, then the G below with your thumb, and the E above with your little finger, all without sounding them. Now find the lowest C on the piano with your left hand, play it loudly and let go. Listen for a moment, and you should be able to hear the three notes G, C and E, even though you did not actually play them.

These notes which vibrate in sympathy with the main note are called *harmonics* or *overtones,* and the timbre of sounds depends partly on the number of harmonics mixed with the main note.

In general, the more overtones or harmonics a sound contains, the richer is its timbre. The flute has a cool, clear sound partly because of the small quantity of its overtones. The piercing, nasal quality of the oboe is due to the peculiar mixture of overtones which the player sets in motion through the reed (a thin piece of cane inserted into the mouthpiece).

All stringed instruments are rich in overtones, whether they are scraped, like the violin family, plucked, like the harp, or struck with hammers, like the piano.

The many different colours or timbres in the orchestra are due to the many different mixtures of harmonics or overtones produced by the various instruments, and to the many ways in which these can be combined.

CHAPTER THREE

How Music Began

ORIGINS · HEBREW AND GREEK MUSIC · MINSTRELS
AND FOLK SONGS · CHURCH MUSIC AND NOTATION

How did music begin? Music is always beginning. Every time you hum, sing or whistle a bit of tune —out of your head—just because you happen to feel like it, you are sowing a seed that could grow into a piece of music.

Every time a savage in the jungle starts drumming his fists on a hollow tree-trunk, he is starting a process that is ages old. For primitive peoples, music is magic — magic that can call up spirits and frighten away wild beasts; magic that can put courage into warriors and give men the feeling of belonging to the tribe; magic that can set the solemn tone of religious rites. With their special kind of drumming, drummers can summon the whole tribe to face some common danger together, or else to take part in ritual dances. In these, by the hypnotic insistence of the rhythmic patterns of their drumming, they can work the dancers up into a frenzy. Sometimes primitive pipes are added to the drums, and there we have a beginning of instrumental music.

Every time a baby coos and chuckles for sheer joy, or cries because it is hungry, it is starting a process that is even older than the drumming and dancing of primeval savages. Cooing, chuckling and crying grow into some kind of speaking. Words are chanted and repeated in a singing voice, making sounds of definite pitch. These odd bits of tune are repeated and balanced, and so folk-songs are born: lullabies, love songs, play songs, work songs, marching songs, dancing songs, praying songs.

All these kinds of music are being created in similar ways all the time, and this has been going on for thousands of years, all over the world.

OUTLINE OF WESTERN MUSIC

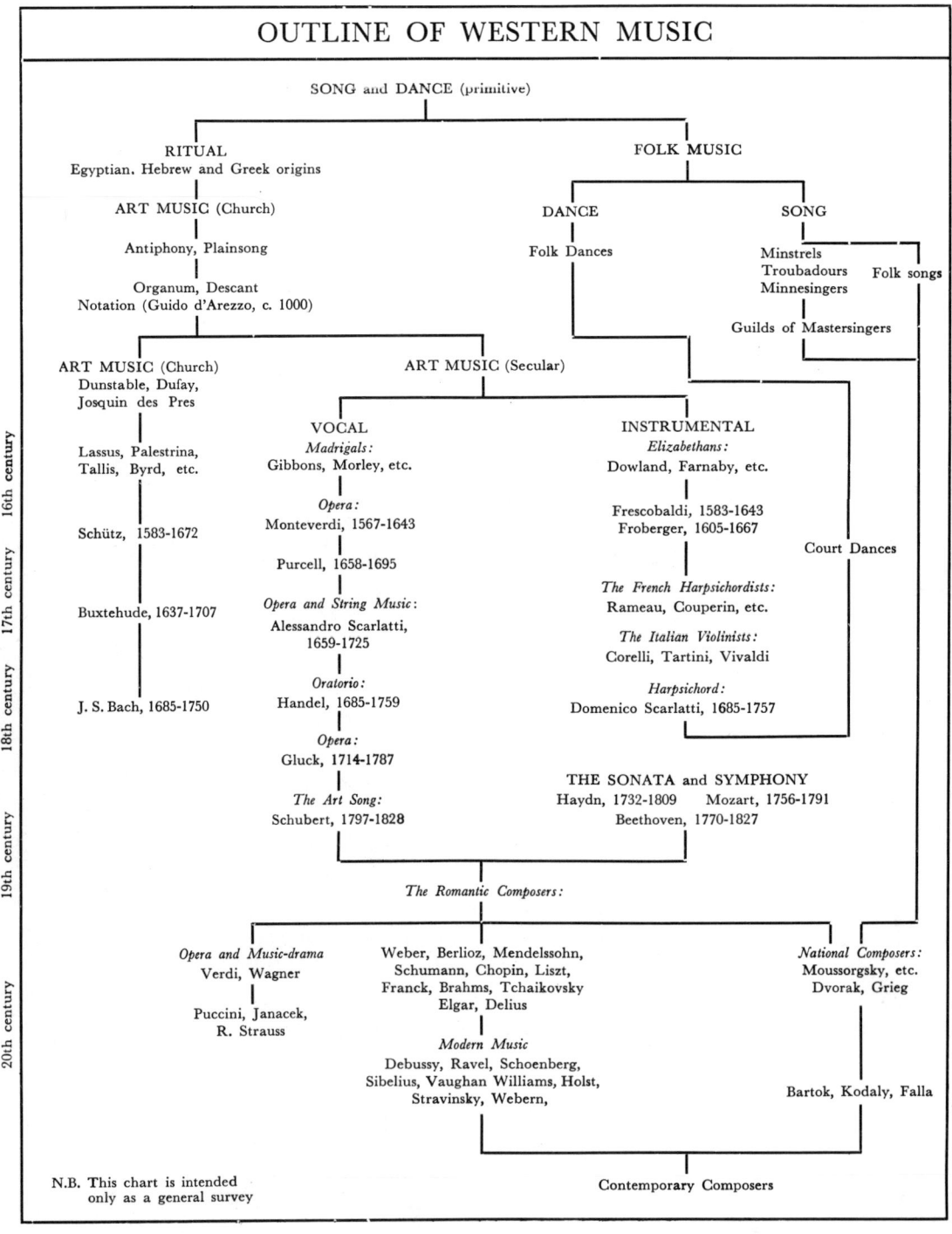

SONG and DANCE (primitive)

RITUAL
Egyptian. Hebrew and Greek origins

FOLK MUSIC

ART MUSIC (Church)

Antiphony, Plainsong

Organum, Descant
Notation (Guido d'Arezzo, c. 1000)

DANCE

Folk Dances

SONG

Minstrels
Troubadours   Folk songs
Minnesingers

Guilds of Mastersingers

ART MUSIC (Church)
Dunstable, Dufay,
Josquin des Pres

ART MUSIC (Secular)

VOCAL
Madrigals:
Gibbons, Morley, etc.

INSTRUMENTAL
Elizabethans:
Dowland, Farnaby, etc.

Lassus, Palestrina,
Tallis, Byrd, etc.

Opera:
Monteverdi, 1567-1643

Frescobaldi, 1583-1643
Froberger, 1605-1667

Court Dances

Schütz, 1583-1672

Purcell, 1658-1695

Opera and String Music:
Alessandro Scarlatti,
1659-1725

The French Harpsichordists:
Rameau, Couperin, etc.

Buxtehude, 1637-1707

The Italian Violinists:
Corelli, Tartini, Vivaldi

Oratorio:
Handel, 1685-1759

Harpsichord:
Domenico Scarlatti, 1685-1757

J. S. Bach, 1685-1750

Opera:
Gluck, 1714-1787

The Art Song:
Schubert, 1797-1828

THE SONATA and SYMPHONY
Haydn, 1732-1809   Mozart, 1756-1791
Beethoven, 1770-1827

The Romantic Composers:

Opera and Music-drama
Verdi, Wagner

Puccini, Janacek,
R. Strauss

Weber, Berlioz, Mendelssohn,
Schumann, Chopin, Liszt,
Franck, Brahms, Tchaikovsky
Elgar, Delius

Modern Music
Debussy, Ravel, Schoenberg,
Sibelius, Vaughan Williams, Holst,
Stravinsky, Webern,

National Composers:
Moussorgsky, etc.
Dvorak, Grieg

Bartok, Kodaly, Falla

N.B. This chart is intended
only as a general survey

Contemporary Composers

16th century   17th century   18th century   19th century   20th century

Most of the music we hear is music of the Western world. Western music is rooted in both folk music and ritual music, especially in the ritual or religious music of the ancient Hebrews and the ancient Greeks, who probably learnt much of their music-making from even older civilisations, such as Egypt and Assyria.

In Bible times music played an important part in the people's lives; we know this because there are many parts of the Bible, especially the Psalms, where music is mentioned. Often the people are invited to "Sing unto the Lord", or to "Praise the Lord" with harp and violin, with drum and dance, with pipe and cymbals. In the school of the prophets in ancient Israel, music was part of the training, for a prophet had to be a musician too. There is also a story in the Bible about Saul going out to find the school of the prophets, and meeting them all coming towards him with their musical instruments in their hands.

At the religious festivals of ancient Greece, too, singing and the playing of instruments were an important part of the ceremonies. The ancient Greeks also investigated the scientific basis of music. Over two thousand years ago, Pythagoras, the great mathematician, discovered the overtones in a musical sound by examining the vibrations of a stretched string. He

Ancient Egyptian musicians

The monochord, as used in Ancient Egypt, showed how notes of different pitch could be produced by shortening the vibrating part of a stretched string, by "stopping" (or pressing) it at certain points

King David, from a medieval painting

then sorted out the various overtones and arranged them into scales. His discoveries had far-reaching effects. People thought that these earthly laws must be a reflection of heavenly laws. They imagined that the vast circling of the stars in their courses must produce what they called "the music of the spheres". Far out in space, each star's lonely journey somehow affected that of every other distant star; as a result of all these remote relationships, criss-crossing throughout the universe, there sounded a fantastic, ethereal harmony. Nobody was ever able to hear this strange and wonderful music, but the idea of its possible existence inspired men to try to create a similar kind of harmony in their own music.

As far as we know, the ancient Greeks' idea of music was limited to a single line of melody, based on the

scales which they had invented or discovered. But men of later ages—to this day—have been fascinated by the old legend of "the music of the spheres", and have tried to bring it to life in the musical language of their time.

We know very little about Western music before modern musical notation was invented, which was over a thousand years after the Greek scales were discovered. But we do know that music played a great part in the people's lives. Singing, dancing and playing are mentioned in the earliest known poetry. Poets, like the Old Testament prophets, had to be musicians too. Perhaps you know

the story of Cadmon, the first poet of the English language. He was inspired with the gift of song at a feast of poets, where a harp was passed round from guest to guest as a matter of course.

The bard or poet would recite his poem, give his news, or sing his mes-

rhythmical was the tune, and the easier it was to remember.

Some of the oldest folk-songs are work songs. A definite rhythmic movement, repeated by a group of people over and over again, would easily be helped by words like "Yo, heave ho!" which were sung almost as

sage, accompanying himself on the harp, making up the music as he went along. This kind of music-making is called "improvisation" or "rhapsody". (It is still done in Wales, where the people are very musical.)

Sometimes the words and music became fixed in a song, which was then handed down from generation to generation, and this is how many folk-songs came about. The more rhythmical the words were, the more

soon as they were spoken. Lullabies and play songs, too, had rhythmical word patterns, short and simple, which were very easy to sing and remember.

In field, cottage and castle, music grew like the wild flowers. But there was one place where music was carefully cultivated. This was the church. A large part of the religious service was based on the singing of Psalms, in which the first phrase was sung by

23

one singer, or group of singers, and the answering phrase was sung by another group of singers. (This is called *antiphony*.) Musicians of the church, as well as the men, women and children of the congregation, were able to remember many tunes by means of the Psalms.

In Europe, the first known attempts at notation were made in about the seventh century for the purpose of singing Psalms. Psalm-singing was kept up by all church singers, one generation learning the tunes by ear from another. In this they were helped by special signs, called *neumes,* written over some of the words, which reminded them of a bit of tune that they already knew, and that went with these words. This is an idea that may have been copied from the Hebrew Bible, which is sung with the help of similar signs to this day. These bits of tune are probably the very same ones as were sung in Solomon's Temple three thousand years ago. Some of them probably passed over into the early Christian Church.

The old tunes used for Psalm-singing are called *plainsong*. Most of them are in special scales called "church modes", and correspond to the scales you can play all on white keys on the piano, starting on any note except B.

Usually the tunes were sung in *unison*—that is to say, all the singers sang the same tune at a pitch which suited their voices, so that the high and low voices were one or two octaves apart, like this:

```
C D F D E D
C D F D E D
C D F D E D
```

But sometimes some of the singers started singing on the wrong note by mistake, and then went on singing the whole tune at the wrong pitch. The effect was not disliked by some of the musicians of the time, and they fixed the possible extra starting note at a fourth below the tune. After that, this was the effect heard:

```
C D F D E D
G A C A B A
C D F D E D
G A C A B A
```

At first it seemed strange, but gradually the people came to like it. It was called *organum*.

Another effect was brought about by lazy singers who could not be bothered to sing the tune, but just kept singing on one note, something like this:

```
C D F D E D
C C C C C C
C D F D E D
C C C C C C
```

This effect was called the *drone,* and must have sounded something like bagpipes, which have one or more drones going on all the time.

As these new ways of singing came about, church music became more and more complicated, and the more complicated the music was, the more urgent became the need for a way of writing music down that would show

24

exactly what the notes were, instead of merely reminding people of tunes they already knew, as the rather vague old neumes did. For hundreds of years, musicians tried various ways of writing music, but musical notation as we know it today is largely due to the ingenuity of an Italian monk, Guido of Arezzo, who lived nearly a thousand years ago.

By giving composers the means of writing down their musical ideas, and performers the means of learning them, Guido opened up a new world of musical activity. He helped musicians and music-lovers in two different ways. On the one hand, he found a way of showing the actual, fixed pitch of sounds — that is, "absolute pitch". On the other hand, he helped people to read music by means of "relative pitch" — that is, the way that the notes of a melody or a scale are related to their home note, without regard to their absolute pitch.

Guido's way of showing the actual pitch of sounds was something like this: first he devised names for the notes of a scale that we would today call C major. For this he used a Latin hymn in which the first line began on what we now call the home note, or tonic, of C major. The next line of this hymn began on the second note of the scale, and so on till the sixth note. Taking the first syllable of each of the six lines of this hymn, this is what he got: *ut re mi fa sol la*. Later

a seventh syllable was added, *si,* and these are the names that have been used in France for the notes of the C major scale ever since. Later the *ut* was changed to *do,* as being easier to sing, and this has been used in Italy and other countries ever since. In England, Germany and neighbouring countries, the letters of the alphabet were later introduced instead of the Latin syllables.

In Guido's day nearly all music— and especially church music—was sung. Guido realised that no single human voice could reach up or down to more than a certain number of notes—usually about twelve. He reckoned that to cover the range of high voices, medium voices and low voices he would need to find a way of writing about twenty-two notes. This he did by ruling eleven lines, making a ladder, or *staff* (or stave), and placing some notes so that the lines went through them, and other notes in the spaces between the lines.

This ladder of eleven lines is usually called the *great staff.* Calling the middle line *ut* (middle C), Guido worked out all the other notes, like this:

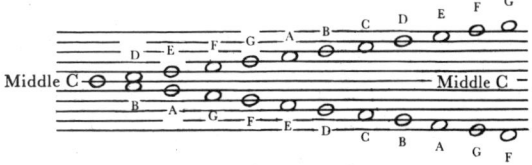

The great staff with note names

Next, realising that no one voice would ever need to use more than a few notes, and therefore only a few lines, Guido invented the *clefs* to show the pitch of the particular lines used:

Treble or G clef

C clef

Bass or F clef

In the course of time the staff came to be fixed at five lines, and this is what we use now. Here is the divided staff with the principal clefs:

Middle C on the treble staff

Middle C on the bass staff

The other equally useful thing that Guido did was inventing a way of helping people to sing tunes at sight. He found that they could quite easily sing a tune at sight if it had *ut* (*do* or C) as the keynote (or home note). But if the keynote was a different note they got confused. In those days only three scales were used, corresponding to C, F and G. Guido suggested that people should sing the syllable *ut* for the keynote even if its actual pitch was F or G, but he warned them to remember that they were actually *transposing* (or shifting) the tune on to sounds of different pitch. This method of sight-singing by means of the movable *ut* or *do,* known as "solmization", is one that has been further developed and widely used in various ways ever since Guido's day, including the popular tonic sol-fa method, to help people who cannot read music from the staff.

When Guido first invented solmization, he demonstrated it to the Pope, who was so interested in it that he then and there sang at sight a tune he had never heard before. The Pope was so delighted at being able to do such a thing that he gave Guido every encouragement for his clever inventions. With the Pope's help and support, Guido was able to get his good ideas spread all over Europe. In this way a new world of music-making was opened up for musicians and music-lovers alike.

LISTEN TO SOME OF THESE RECORDS

African Drumming: Congo and Tutsi Drums. *Indian Work Songs:* Rice Transplanting Song; Marathi Weavers' Song. *Jewish Sacred Music:* Psalm 8. *Ancient Greek Music:* First Delphic Hymn. *Plainsong, (Gregorian Antiphonal Psalmody):* Domine in virtute.

CHAPTER FOUR

Reading and Writing Music

NOTATION OF RHYTHM   ·   NOTATION OF PITCH   ·
TEMPO AND DYNAMICS   ·   SIGHT-READING   ·   BASIC
TABLES

Would you like to learn how to read music? It can be quite fun, especially if you learn to write it at the same time. You will need a sheet of music paper, a pencil and a rubber.

Let us start like this: sing the first verse of *What shall we do with a drunken sailor?*, at the same time clapping or tapping the rhythmic pattern. Now sing the first phrase only, rather slowly, while you write one dot for each sound, on any one line of your music paper, like this:

Now make them into nice, round dots:

And add a short stroke, like a stem, to each one, like this:

Now you have written ten *notes*.

Sing the first line of the song again, pointing to one note for every sound you sing. You will notice that you have to go quickly from the second note to the third, for the words "shall we", and from the fifth to the sixth notes, for the words "with a". Join up those two pairs of notes with a little line, like this:

Now sing it again, beating time to find out where *one* comes. You will find that it is in four-time. Put a vertical line in front of each *one*, like this:

This is called a *bar-line*, and the space between two bar-lines is called a *bar*. You have now written two bars.

Write the next phrase of the song in the same way. And the next. Both the second and third phrases have exactly the same rhythmic pattern as the first. What about the last phrase of the song? There you have two longer sounds for "morn-ing", each one lasting for two beats. Make them like this:

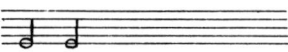

Here is your rhythmic pattern complete:

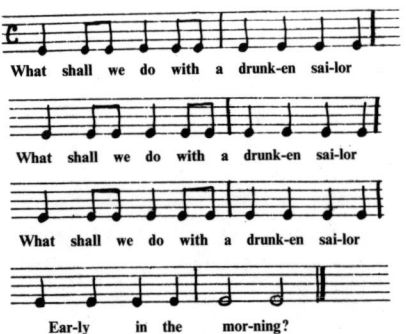

The **C** at the beginning stands for *common time,* which means four-time, or four beats in each bar.

You don't need bar-lines at the beginning of each line of music, because we naturally assume that the first note is *one*. (But see p. 12.)

The double bar-line at the end shows that this is the end of the piece.

These notes are called *crotchets:*

These notes are called *quavers:*

These notes are called *minims:*

So much for the rhythm. But now what about the pitch?

The pitch of a note is shown by its place on the staff, and the G clef at the beginning shows which line G would be written on:

Can you work out where the other notes would be written? F would be just one step lower than G, and as G is on a line, F should be in the next space below, like this:

then E would be on the line below that:

and D would be just under the staff, like this:

Practise writing all the notes out from D to the next D, like this:

(We turn the stems down instead of up halfway up the staff, because it looks neater.)

Now we are ready to write the pitch of our song. The first thing to do is to write a G clef. Never mind if you can't make it the proper shape at first, so long as you make it end clearly on the G line—like this:

Our song begins on A (see p. 14), which is just one note higher than the starting-point of the G clef.

There are seven A's at the beginning of this tune, so let us write them all down, with the right rhythm:

Sing the tune again, pointing to each of the notes you have written. Stop! Sing the second bar slowly. Do you recognise it as a chord tune? It uses the notes of a minor triad: the chord

A
F
D

Pick out the notes in the right order and write them down in your second bar. Your tune should now look like this:

The curved line under the two bars is called a *phrase mark,* and it shows that all these notes belong to one phrase.

You may remember that the second phrase of this song is the same shape as the first; that is to say, it has exactly the same rhythmic pattern, and the pitch goes up and down in the same places; that is, the first bar consists of repeated notes and the second bar is a chord tune. But the second phrase does not begin on the same note as the first one did, it begins one note lower, on the G, and the second chord tune is not a minor triad, but a major triad, the chord

G
E
C

Once you have noticed this, it should be quite easy to work out the second phrase, which should now look like this:

These two phrases together form what is called a *sequence*—that is, one phrase followed by another (or more than one) similar phrase at a slightly different pitch.

The third phrase begins like the first, and the rhythm is the same all through, but after the first note in the second bar the pitch takes a turn in a different direction, walking up step by step (a scale tune), very easy to write, simply A B C D.

29

It may take you a little time to work out the fourth phrase, "Early in the morn-ing". It starts one note down from the last note of the third phrase, on C (see p. 29), then, singing down the scale (see p. 28), and picking out the notes of the tune, you get A, G, then, missing one out again, you get E, then, finally, two D's. So here is your last phrase, with a so-called double bar to show it is the end.

Now you are nearly ready to sing the song from the *manuscript* (which means "written by hand"). But not quite. We need something to show the tempo. Tempo indications are usually written in Italian. Do you want it fast or slow? Fast? Very fast or fairly fast? If you want it very fast, write *presto* (*press*-toh) over the beginning of the first bar. If you want it only fairly fast, write *allegro* (al-*lay*-groh). If you want it at a walking pace, write *andante* (an-*dan*-tay). If you want it a moderate pace, write *moderato* (mo-de-*rah*-to).

Now what about the dynamics? Choose either of these:

f for *forte* (*for*-tay), meaning "loud".

p for *piano* (pee-*ah*-noh), meaning "soft" (or any others from the table of dynamics on p. 31).

You can use either of these (or any others) in any part of the song, but it is usually better to keep to one of them for a whole phrase.

If you want the music to swell up or to die down, you can use these signs:

(Musicians sometimes call them "hair-pins".) *Crescendo* (cray-*shen*-doh) means "growing", or getting louder, and *diminuendo* (dee-mee-noo-*en*-doh) means "diminishing", or getting softer.

What does the song look like now?

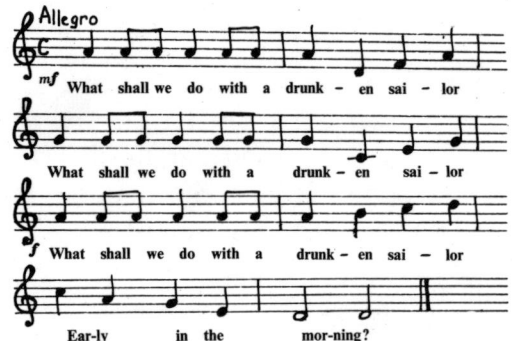

Very good. What about singing it from your manuscript? Begin by beating time (four in a bar) in the right tempo. Then sing it with the right dynamics.

Now that you have sung a song that you have written down yourself, try to sing the tune below. Begin by beating time for a few bars in the right tempo. Then clap the rhythm, making sure you clap the crotchets evenly, with a slight accent on the first of each bar, and that you wait long enough on the minims — that is, two full beats each time. By the time you get to the quavers, you will probably have recognised the tune. Do you recognise it?

The sign   on the B line stands for flat, and it means that every B in this piece must be B flat, because this piece is in the scale, or *key,* of F major.

Now sing this tune to "lah", pointing to each note as you sing it. You may say you don't know how to find the first note. In that case you could find it by playing the F above middle C on the piano (or any other instrument).

When you have finished singing this tune from the page, you will have done what is called *sight-reading,* or singing at sight.

Some people can find the pitch of any note in their heads; we say that they have absolute pitch. It is a very useful gift, but not all musicians have it. What we all have, whether we are musicians or not, is relative pitch; that is to say, when we hear a tune we naturally hear how one note is related to another. This is why we can learn tunes by ear, and partly why we can remember them.

Now you are nearly ready to try to sight-read some of the tunes in the other chapters of this book. But first, here are some tables which you may find useful.

SOME INDICATIONS OF TEMPO, ETC.

Adagio (a-*dah*-jo), slow
Allegretto (al-lay-*gret*-to), fairly lively
Allegro (al-*lay*-gro), fast
Andante (an-*dan*-tay), fairly slow
Assai (a-*ssah*-i), rather
Ben marcato (mar-*cah*-to), well accented
Brioso (bree-*oh*-so), vigorous
Con moto (*moh*-to), with movement
Dolce (*dol*-chay), sweet
Espressivo (es-pre-*ssee*-vo), expressively
Larghetto (lar-*get*-toh), slow and steady
Largo (*lar*-goh), broad (very slow)
Lento (*len*-toh), slow
Legato (le-*gah*-to), smoothly
Maestoso (mah-yes-*toh*-so), majestically
Moderato (mo-de-*rah*-to), at a moderate pace
Molto (*moll*-to), very
Morendo (mo-*ren*-do), dying away
Non troppo (*trop*-po), not too much
Pesante (pay-*zan*-tay), heavily
Prestissimo (pres-*tiss*-i-mo), very fast indeed
Presto (*press*-to), very fast

Rit. = ritenuto (rit-en-*oo*-to), held back, getting slower
Scherzando (skair-*tsan*-do), playfully
Tempo giusto (*tem*-po *joos*-to), strict time
Vivace (vee-*vah*-chay), vivacious
Vivo (*vee*-vo), lively

SOME INDICATIONS OF DYNAMICS

cresc. crescendo (cray-*shen*-do), getting louder
dim. diminuendo (dee-mee-noo-*en*-do), getting softer
f = *forte* (*fawr*-tay), loud
ff = *fortissimo* (fawr-*tiss*-i-mo), very loud
fp = *forte-piano,* first loud, then soft
fz = *forzato* (fawr-*tsah*-to), forced
mf = *mezzo forte* (met-so-*fawr*-tay), fairly loud
mp = *mezzo piano* (*pyah*-no), fairly soft
p = *piano* (*pyah*-no), soft
pp = *pianissimo* (pya-*niss*-i-mo), very soft
rf = *rinforzando* (rin-fawr-*tsan*-do), reinforced, suddenly louder
sf = *sforzando* (sfawr-*tsan*-do), suddenly loud
sfp = *sforzando-piano,* suddenly loud, then soft

31

PITCH

STAFF AND CLEFS

 Treble clef, used for all high voices and all instruments with a range from about Middle C upwards.

 Soprano clef, used for the upper voice in early music. (see page 47)

 Alto clef, sometimes called the *Viola clef;* used for the viola; and for the middle voice in early music. (see page 64)

 Tenor clef, used for the tenor trombone; for the cello and bassoon in their higher registers; and for the tenor voice in early music.

 Bass clef, used for all low voices and all instruments with a range from about Middle C downwards.

 Combined *Treble and Bass clefs,* used for all keyboard instruments (e.g., piano, harpsichord and organ) and the harp.

Note names on combined staff with ledger lines

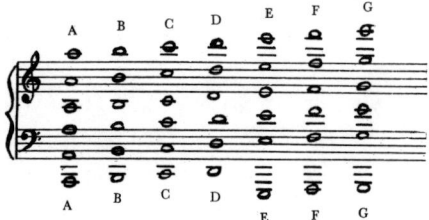

Here are most of the notes used in music. For still higher notes the sign *8va* is used, meaning an octave higher. For still lower notes the sign *8va bassa* is used, meaning an octave lower. (see page 98)

INTERVALS

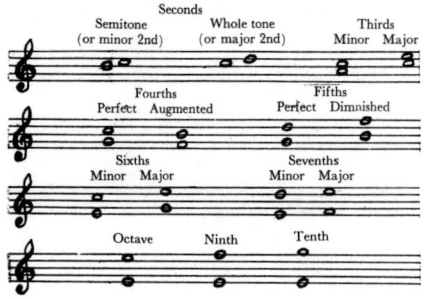

ACCIDENTALS

♯ = Sharp = 1 semitone higher

♭ = Flat = 1 semitone lower

✗ = Double sharp = 2 semitones higher

♭♭ = Double flat = 2 semitones lower

♮ = Natural = note at normal pitch

SCALES AND CHORDS

Degrees of the scale:

I = Keynote, Home-note, TONIC or *Doh;* II = SUPERTONIC or *Ray;* III = MEDIANT or *Me;* IV = SUBDOMINANT or *Fah;* V = DOMINANT or *Soh;* VI = SUBMEDIANT or *Lah;* VII = LEADING NOTE or *Te.*

32

RHYTHM

NOTES

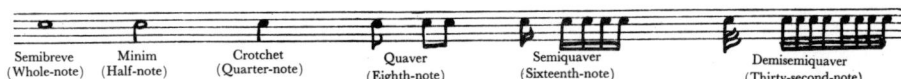

Semibreve (Whole-note)   Minim (Half-note)   Crotchet (Quarter-note)   Quaver (Eighth-note)   Semiquaver (Sixteenth-note)   Demisemiquaver (Thirty-second-note)

A semibreve rest is also used for a whole bar's rest, whatever the time signature.

RESTS

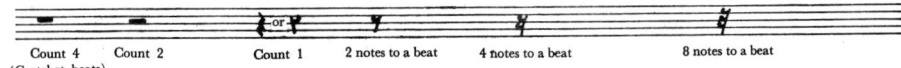

Count 4   Count 2   Count 1   2 notes to a beat   4 notes to a beat   8 notes to a beat
(Crotchet beats)

A dot after a note makes it half as long again, e.g.,

A tie between 2 notes of the same pitch adds the durations together, e.g.,

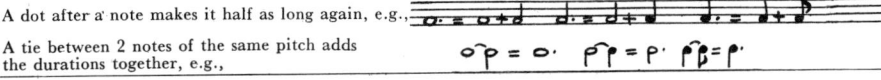

USUAL TIME SIGNATURES

$\frac{4}{4}$ or C = Common time = 4 crotchets in a bar

$\frac{2}{2}$ or ¢ = Alla breve = 2 minims in a bar

$\frac{2}{4}$ = 2 crotchets in a bar

$\frac{3}{4}$ = 3 crotchets in a bar

$\frac{3}{8}$ = 3 quavers in a bar

$\frac{6}{8}$ = 2 dotted crotchets (or 6 quavers) in a bar

$\frac{9}{8}$ = 3 dotted crotchets (or 9 quavers) in a bar

$\frac{12}{8}$ = 4 dotted crotchets (or 12 quavers) in a bar

OTHER TIME SIGNATURES

$\frac{3}{2}$ = 3 minims in a bar

$\frac{6}{4}$ = 2 dotted minims (or 6 crotchets) in a bar

$\frac{9}{4}$ = 3 dotted minims (or 9 crotchets) in a bar

$\frac{5}{4}$ = 5 crotchets in a bar

$\frac{7}{4}$ = 7 crotchets in a bar

$\frac{5}{8}$ = 5 quavers in a bar

$\frac{8}{8}$ = 8 quavers in a bar

$\frac{3}{16}$ = 3 semiquavers in a bar

Clap the rhythm of these songs before you try to sing them:

Early One Morning

God Save the Queen

All Through the Night

Glory, Glory, Alleluia

The Bluebells of Scotland

Oh where tell me where is your Highland laddie gone?

Charlie is my Darling

Dashing Away with a Smoothing Iron

D'ye Ken John Peel

33

CHAPTER FIVE

How Music Grew

ENGLAND: VOCAL POLYPHONY, MADRIGALS, VIRGINAL
MUSIC, VARIATIONS · PURCELL · HANDEL
FRANCE: COURT DANCES, HARPSICHORD MUSIC,
ITALY: OPERA AND ORATORIO, THE VIOLINISTS
GERMANY: THE CHORALE, THE ORGAN, FUGUE · J. S. BACH

THIS INTRIGUING MANUSCRIPT, the Reading Rota, is over seven hundred years old. It is a song known to most English schoolboys and girls as *Summer is a-coming in*. This is how it begins:

While heralding the summer in a most inviting way, this remarkable composition did far more — it also heralded the full flowering of art music that gradually came about after notation was invented.

It is interesting for several reasons. To begin with, it is not only a very good tune in itself; it is a round (in Latin, *rota*) or *canon*; that is to say, the singers start singing this song one after the other (as in *Frère Jacques)*, and the tune is so cleverly composed

The Reading Rota: Sumer is icumen in, ascribed to John of Fornsete, a monk of Reading Abbey in the thirteenth century

that everything fits. Not only this, but in the *Reading Rota* two lower voices sing another (shorter) tune at the same time, and this not only fits the other canon, but is itself in canon! As a result of all this, there are six different tunes being sung together at any moment of the performance. This kind of many-voiced music is called *polyphony* (pol-*if*-on-i).

It is a far cry from the single melodic strands of plainsong, where only one tune is heard at a time, to the elaborate weavings of polyphony, where several different tunes are heard at the same time. Nobody knows quite how or where polyphony came about, but one of the earliest records we have of it is the *Reading Rota*.

Some people think that John of Fornsete was merely using his skill in notation in order to record a folksong of his time. It is possible that he adapted this song to a style of singing that may have been known only to church musicians. On the other hand, it seems quite likely that folk-singers might have hit on the novel effect of starting a song at different times entirely by chance. Have you ever tried singing a song to an echo? You could imagine someone singing up in the hills and hearing the sounds echoed back, and liking the effect so much that he told his friends about it and tried to copy it. However that may be, the fact remains that here was a

church musician writing down a folksong of great artistry.

For us, looking back on that remote age, when art music was in its infancy, the *Reading Rota* is an exciting sign of the living bond between the cultivated art of the Church and the spontaneous music-making of the people.

There are many reminders of folk-music in the church music of the Middle Ages. Some early polyphonic Psalm settings sound very like folk-songs. Here is the tune of one:

Alleluia Psallat (anonymous)

Also there are hidden folk-songs in some of the most solemn compositions of that time, in which the basic tune was a popular song of the day, in disguise, sung so slowly as to be unrecognisable!

One of the first great composers of polyphonic music that we know of was an Englishman, John of Dunstable, who lived in the fifteenth century. He made an important addition to the vocabulary of church music by using the intervals of thirds and sixths, which until then had been banned in church music, though they had been used in folk music for hundreds of years, on account of their naturally harmonious effect. Here are a few bars of music by Dunstable, to give you a little idea of its flavour:

Moderato

"Alleluia", closing bars of Quam Pulchra Es

Dunstable's teachings and compositions had a far-reaching effect, and the following century saw the birth of some of the greatest composers of all time: Palestrina in Italy, Lassus in the Netherlands, Tallis and Byrd in England. All these composers were

Thomas Tallis (1505-1585) and William Byrd (1543-1623), the great composers of England's Golden Age of music

very great artists, and they wrote exquisite polyphonic music to be sung in churches. Their masses and motets (compositions with religious texts, usually in Latin) are not easy to understand at a first hearing, partly because there are so many independent tunes going on at the same time; but the more you listen to this music, the more you will understand and enjoy it. If you can borrow some gramophone records of this kind of music,

listen to a little at a time, over and over again, trying to pick out the tune in the different voices. It is a good idea to listen sometimes to the highest voice, sometimes to the lowest, and sometimes to pick out the middle one. (See list of records, p. 49.)

These composers, and many others, also composed some equally exquisite songs for the entertainment of music-lovers out of church hours. They made many vocal settings, in polyphonic style, of poems by some of the most famous poets of the day. These songs were called *madrigals.* You may know one of them: *It was a lover and his lass*; the words are by Shakespeare and the music is by Thomas Morley. It begins like this:

Fast

England in the first Elizabethan age was indeed a fountain of music-making. Madrigals were sung in every home where there were educated people. They gathered round a table to sing the madrigals at sight, and for this purpose the music sheets were printed with each voice-part facing a different way, so that it could be comfortably seen by each singer.

Besides vocal music, people began to be interested in instrumental music. The first Queen Elizabeth is said to have been an accomplished player on the virginals, a small keyboard instrument in which the strings were

36

From the madrigal The Silver Swan *by Orlando Gibbons (1583-1625)*

songs, and the melodies of songs were often played on recorders and viols. Some composers headed their compositions "Apt for Voyces or Viols", giving people the choice of either singing or playing them.

Many charming pieces were specially composed for virginals, some of the most attractive ones by Giles Farnaby; these not only had quaint, fanciful names, like *Giles Farnaby's Dreame, His Rest, His Conceit*, etc., but also a delightful freshness and humour as of folk-songs and dances. If you can play the piano a little, you ought to be able to play some of these quite easily.

Tower Hill *by Giles Farnaby (about 1560 - about 1600)*

plucked by quills attached to the keys. She set a fashion which was followed throughout the country and lasted until long after her reign was over. Virginals were so popular that they were found not only in almost every household, but even in barbers' shops, where "barbers' virginals" were provided for customers to play on while waiting for attention. It is touching to read of the attempts people made, in the Great Fire of London, to salvage their virginals by throwing them into the Thames barges along with other of their most treasured possessions.

Other instruments were popular too, such as recorders, lutes and viols. Lutes were used chiefly to accompany

What could be more natural, after playing a delightful tune, than to repeat it? And having repeated it, how natural to repeat it again and again, playing it a little differently each time. Pieces composed in this way are called *variations*. In those days they were sometimes called "divisions", because in each new variation the notes were divided into shorter ones: minims became crotchets, crotchets became quavers, these became semiquavers, and so on. In this way the

The virginals, a small keyboard instrument

music became more and more elaborate as it went along (see p. 41).

(see p. 41)

Some composers of the time wrote pieces for the virginals with as many as forty-four variations. However, these were not intended to be played all together, but to give the player plenty of choice, according to his mood and taste.

In the middle of the seventeenth century there were drastic changes in musical England. The Puritans, Cromwell among them, objected to the elaborate music-making in the churches, and they disbanded many church choirs. They also forbade public music-making, and many theatres were closed. Some composers became schoolmasters; by teaching music in the schools they helped to keep interest in music alive. But soon after the restoration of the monarchy, when the choir of the Chapel Royal was restored too, there appeared some very gifted choirboys, who not only sang like angels but also showed remarkable talent for composition. One of the most gifted of these boys, Pelham Humfrey, was sent to Paris for three years to study, under Lully, the new musical fashions from Italy which were all the rage in Paris at that time. He returned to England a "compleat Monsieur" (as Pepys wrote in his famous diary), but besides the airs and graces of a French gentleman, Humfrey brought with him some exciting new musical ideas. Unfortunately, he died very young—only twenty-seven —but his vivid compositions brought new life to musical England.

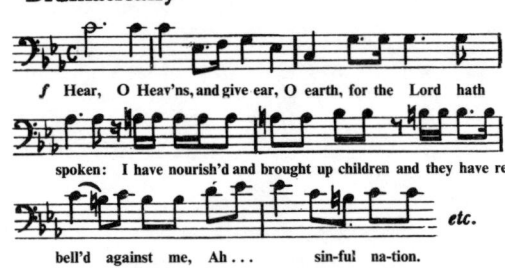

Hear, O Heavens *by Pelham Humfrey*
(1647 - 1674)

First to profit by this fresh knowledge and outlook was Henry Purcell, a younger fellow-choirboy of Pelham Humfrey's. It was not long before Purcell proved himself a most extraordinary and original genius and in due course he came to be recognised as the crown and pride of English music. During his short life—he died in his thirties—an enormous number of varied compositions flowed from his

38

Henry Purcell (1659-1695)

flowed from him with hardly a pause for breath, as if he sensed the shortness of his days and could not bear to waste them.

A large part of Purcell's enormous output, both grave and gay, was written for the theatre, where it was the fashion to produce plays and masques with incidental music (that is, music performed during a play). His most beautiful work for the theatre is *Dido and Aeneas,* an opera (see p. 43), originally written for a girls' school in London. It includes one of Purcell's best-known airs: Dido's lament, *When I am laid in earth.* This touching song is written with what is known as a "ground bass" accompaniment, that is, a tune in the bass that recurs over and over again. In this case Purcell uses a favourite device of his, a ground bass moving down in semitones.

pen. (It would take an ordinary person a lifetime merely to copy them out!) Glorious choral music for the church and intimate vocal and instrumental music for the home; jubilant music for royal occasions and solemn music for funerals; all these

The ground bass is written in larger notes than the rest

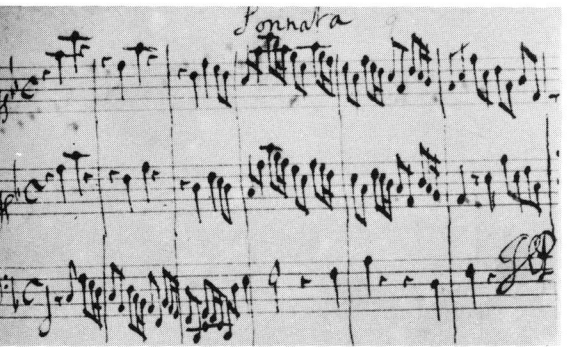

Purcell's so-called Golden Sonata *(see page 61) in his own writing*

Many years later this same device

was used by J. S. Bach as a basis for one of the most solemn passages in all music :

Ground bass from "Crucifixus" from the Mass in B minor

After Purcell died, there was no one in England who could compare with him, and English music went entirely out of fashion. Only foreign music and musicians were applauded with any enthusiasm.

Among the many musicians who were attracted to England from the Continent, there was one who became so much a part of English musical life that his German origins were almost forgotten. This was Handel. Having left the land of his birth when he was twenty-one and spent several years in Italy, Handel then came to England quite by chance. He was so pleased with his welcome and he liked England so much that in due course he settled down in London for good. Here he wrote many beautiful operas in the Italian language and style. But in time the people in England began to get tired of Italian operas based on ancient Greek myths and medieval romances, and they much preferred Handel's oratorios (see p. 43), for these were sung in English and were based on the Bible stories they knew

and loved. The most famous of Handel's oratorios are *Israel in Egypt* and *Messiah,* especially the latter, which is performed regularly all over Britain.

Handel's music is full of good tunes. Truth to tell, some of them were copied from other composers. Handel thought nothing of using a good tune, wherever he had heard it; it was the custom in those days. Besides, the basic tunes of the fashionable music of the time were so simple and straightforward that one could find the same or similar tunes being used by several composers. Many of Handel's tunes are simple chord tunes or simple scale tunes in clear, strong rhythms. Here are some typical fragments of Handelian melody:

From Samson

From Messiah

From Organ Concerto in F, *op. 4, no. 4*

What mattered was not so much the tune itself as what the composer did with it. Handel had a special gift for making "great effects with simple

George Frideric Handel (1685-1759) is usually portrayed with full wig (like Couperin shown on p. 43). Here Handel is seen dressed informally, and as he probably looked while composing

What had been going on in France all this time?

In complete contrast to the freely flowing music of England's Golden Age, the picture presented by France under Louis XIV in the next century (the seventeenth) was a very different one. There everything was severely restricted by the rigid formalities of the Court. Music, like everything else, was carefully directed to suit the refined tastes of the "Sun King", as Louis XIV was called, and the lords and ladies of his retinue.

In the Court of the "Sun King", ballet played a great part, with Lully as its first and foremost composer. The King even danced in the ballets himself, and he employed what was then considered a large number of musicians to provide the music. At one time there were as many as twenty-four instruments of the violin family

means", as Beethoven said many years later; and Haydn said, when he first heard the Hallelujah Chorus of the *Messiah*, "He is the master of us all!"

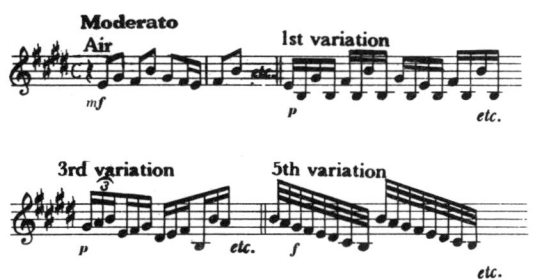

Air with variations from Suite in E

Handel's harpsichord

in his orchestra. Many of the dances, such as the minuet and the gavotte, and much of the music that accompanied them, came originally from the French countryside. But they soon lost their simple peasant quality in the artificial atmosphere of the Royal Court, and before long they were copied, in their formal disguise, in all the courts of Europe, where their country origins were forgotten.

In France, too, much fine music was written for the harpsichord, a larger and more powerful instrument than the delicately-toned English virginals. The French harpsichordists, chief among them Couperin and Rameau, composed many pieces in the style of the Court dances. They also invented a form (or musical shape) based on an old type of French poem, the *rondeau,* in which the first tune returned again and again with contrasting sections in between.

Keyboard music of the sixteenth and seventeenth centuries is simply peppered with ornaments or "grace notes". Some people think this is because the short, plucked sounds of the harpsichord seemed rather bare unless they were decked out with trills and trimmings. But it is just as likely that people dressed up their music for the same reasons as they dressed themselves in frills and furbelows, embroideries and lace ruffles: because that was the fashion of their day, and they liked it.

Minuet in F *by Purcell. (The notes in the bracket show how the trill should be played)*

A speciality of the French harpsichordists was the writing of descriptive music, such as *Le Coucou,* by Daquin, in which the notes of the cuckoo's call are woven into the whole of the piece. Another example of this type of composition is *La Poule,* by Rameau, a most excellent piece of music which is at the same time a most lifelike imitation of a clucking hen.

La Poule *by Rameau (1683-1764)*

Couperin, the greatest of them all, wrote dozens of pieces of pictorial music with titles like *Le Tic-toc-choc* (the ticking clock), *Les Petits Moulins à Vent* (the little windmills) and many others.

Le Tic Toc Choc *by Couperin*

Italy, the land of golden voices, has always specialised in vocal music. Something in the air of Italy seems to make it as natural for Italians to sing as to breathe. Both the *opera* and the *oratorio* originally came from Italy, where they were first created in about 1600. An opera is a play with music in which the actors sing their parts. The orchestra is used to accompany the singers and to emphasise dramatic situations. An oratorio is a similar kind of composition, but it is always based on some religious subject, and it is only sung, not acted. There is also the *cantata* (an Italian word meaning "something sung"), which can be either a short oratorio or else a miniature opera, not acted.

All these vocal compositions—cantata, opera and oratorio—were based on a new style of singing called *recitative,* which, as its name suggests, was a cross between reciting and singing. It was invented by a group of Italian composers who were fired with the

François Couperin (1668-1733), called "Couperin le Grand" (the great), to distinguish him from the other composers in his family

idea of re-creating the style in which, as they thought, the ancient Greeks had performed their dramas. The vocal line followed the natural expression of the words, which also provided the rhythm.

(To get some idea of how this was done, make a short remark—anything will do—repeat it, notice the rhythm of it and write it down. Then say it again, noticing how your voice rises and falls. Now say it again in more of a singing voice; if you have the patience to go to the piano and find out the notes you are singing and write them down with the right rhythm, you will have written a piece of recitative!)

Accompaniment was provided by chords played now and again, usually on the harpsichord. Here is an example of the effect from Handel's *Messiah*:

Recitative

As well as the recitatives, these vocal compositions always included some formal songs. In the course of most operas, oratorios and cantatas, there were moments when the story would stop while one singer expressed his feelings in a song. These songs were written in a special form called the *da capo aria* (da-*cah*-po *ar*-yah), so named because it consisted of a first air (tune) and then a second air, at the end of which were the words *Da capo al fine* (*fee*-nay), indicating that the first air should be sung again to finish up with. Many beautiful melodies were written in this form, but the accompaniments were usually quite simple. Gone were the elaborate melodic weavings of the polyphonic age. The instrumental accompaniments were now so straightforward that they could be reduced to basic chords which could be indicated in a kind of shorthand called *figured bass*.

Though accompaniments to recitatives were usually played on the harpsichord, many other instruments were used to accompany the arias and to provide an introduction, interludes and the *finale* (fee-*nah*-lay), an ending-off piece. The orchestras of the seventeenth century consisted chiefly of bowed instruments, such as viols and violins. The Italians made such wonderful violins that these gradually took the place of the instruments of the older viol family. Side by side with the great Italian violin-makers are the great Italian violinist-composers: Corelli, Vivaldi, Tartini and a host of others, for whose wonderful playing some of these superb instruments were probably made.

All this time there had been a wealth of music-making going on in Germany and Austria, though their Golden Age was yet to come. Music-lovers today are so dominated by the greatness of Bach and Handel, Mozart and Beethoven, that they are apt to forget the richly musical background in which these composers were brought up. The German-speaking people were always lovers of music. In the field of folk-music, bards

44

and minstrels had their counterpart in Germany, where the "Master-singers", as some of the German min-strels were called, formed themselves into guilds, like other craftsmen of the time. The contests staged among them were exciting events in the people's lives.

Like their Italian neighbours over the Alps and their English contem-poraries over the sea, the German people regarded music-making as an essential part of their everyday lives from the Middle Ages onward. A strong move to popularise German religious music was made by Martin Luther, who, in the sixteenth century, introduced simple hymns into church and home, so that even the least edu-cated people could join in the church music on Sundays and holy-days. This type of hymn was called a *chorale,* and it played an important part in many of the compositions of the time and later.

From Bach's St. Matthew Passion

The organ, too, played an impor-tant part in German music. Pedals were added to organs in Germany three hundred years before they were introduced into England, thus en-abling the organist to add an extra part to the music with his feet. It was al-most like having a third hand to play the bass with. Northern Germany, in particular, produced a number of great organists in the seventeenth cen-tury.

About that time there was a re-markable family in Germany whose name was Bach. So many members of this family were professional music-ians that for a time the word "Bach" was sometimes used to denote a pro-fessional musician. The greatest of them all—in fact, in some ways the greatest musician who ever lived—was Johann Sebastian Bach. All his life the organ meant a great deal to him; as a boy of fifteen he walked sixty miles to hear a famous organist, and fifteen years later he travelled two hundred miles to hear Buxtehude, the greatest organist of his time—we might add: except himself! Bach was said to be particularly nimble with his feet at the organ. Certainly the pedals are kept pretty busy in his own organ compositions, which include some of his richest and most exciting music.

J. S. Bach was born in the same part of North Germany as Handel, and in the same year, 1685. But whereas Handel was a man of the world and was known all over Europe, Bach never left his native soil. He was a devout citizen and a dedicated crafts-man, working all his life, as the anony-mous artists of the Middle Ages had done, for no personal fame or recognition, but solely "to the glory of God". In his lifetime word got round that Bach was the greatest organist of his day, but his true significance as a composer was only revealed to music-lovers many years after his death, when Mendelssohn discovered and performed his *St. Matthew Passion*, which contains some of the most moving music ever written.

Violin solo from the St. Matthew Passion

Though Bach took a great interest in the music that was being composed in other countries, and even took the trouble to copy out whole works by other composers in order to learn from them, his own art was deeply rooted in the music of the polyphonic age. Throughout his life Bach wrote music for the church: nearly three hundred church cantatas, as well as his other choral works, which include the sublime *Mass in B minor*. But he also wrote instrumental music of many kinds, and even when writing very simple music, such as the little keyboard pieces for Anna Magdalena, his young wife, Bach nearly always wrote them in separate, independent voices. Thus they could easily be sung or played by two or more persons,

Johann Sebastian Bach (1685-1750), here portrayed with part of his family

Prelude in E flat from The Forty-Eight, *in Bach's own writing. (Notice his use of the soprano clef; the first two notes are G and B flat)*

one to each part or voice, with never a dull moment for any of them.

Minuet in A minor

Bach was a devoted father. He had twenty children, some of whom grew up to be fine musicians, thanks to their father's training. As you may imagine, he needed a good many teaching pieces. These he wrote himself, from the easiest pieces for beginners to the most difficult ones for very skilled players. Like nearly all his compositions, his keyboard music soared far beyond its original modest purposes. Wherever in the world Western music is loved and studied and taken seriously, there Bach is the basis and backbone of music-making to this day.

Much of Bach's keyboard music was intended for the clavichord, a tiny keyboard instrument in which the strings were pressed by metal tongues instead of being plucked by quills as they were in the virginals and harpsichord; thus the clavichord can be thought of as the forerunner of the modern piano. Bach invented a new way of tuning the clavichord and the harpsichord so that they could be used for playing music written in any of the twenty-four major and minor keys (see table, p. 32). Before this, keyboard instruments had been tuned in such a way that only a few of the major and minor keys sounded right. In order to provide music for the newly tuned instruments, Bach wrote forty-eight preludes and fugues, called *The Well-tempered Clavier,* meaning the equally-tuned keyboard instrument. In England, this work is affectionately known as *The Forty-eight.*

Whatever he undertook, Bach carried out to perfection. The six *Brandenburg* concertos, in which groups of solo instruments alternate with the orchestra, are a never-ending source of delight, for they abound in good tunes and are full of life and energy. Besides these, Bach wrote many other concertos for various solo instruments. His writing for stringed instruments made especially good use of their characteristic features, such as playing across the strings (see p. 77), as it does in the following example:

From the Double Concerto *for two violins and orchestra*

Bach wrote much of his music, both choral and instrumental, in a style known as *fugue*, which grew out of the old canon (see p. 34). In most of Bach's fugues a single idea—a single tune—dominates the music. The voices first sing the tune, or fugue *subject*, in canon—that is, one after the other. *A counter-subject* acts as a foil to the main tune and helps to bring out its character. After the *exposition* —that is to say, after the first entry of all the voices, there may be an *episode,* during which the music may move into other keys. After that the voices discuss the tune, or subject, between them in various ways. There may be

inversion, the subject turned upside down; *augmentation,* the subject played twice as slow; *diminution,* the subject played twice as fast—all for variety. Then, when the fugue works up towards a climax, you may get *stretto,* where the voices follow one another with the subject in swift imitation, without waiting for each other to finish (like everyone trying to talk at once!). Or there may be a *pedal point,* usually on the dominant or tonic (but not always), where a low note is held on while the other voices excitedly discuss the subject, often in stretto. Finally, when the subject is heard for the last time, it often has a tremendous effect of rounding off the whole fugue.

All these examples are from The Forty-eight:

Subject of Fugue in G major (book I)

Inversion of the subject

The upper voice is the subject of the Fugue in C minor (book II). The lower voice is the subject in augmentation

Stretto from Fugue in G minor (book I). The larger notes show the subject in stretto

Allegro moderato

Tonic pedal from Fugue in C minor (book I)

Try to listen to a Bach fugue on a gramophone record, and see how many of these features you can notice.

We can imagine Bach sitting in his favourite organ loft, listening to the unending stream of melody set in motion by his own playing, and echoing round the beautiful old church. Perhaps he may have been inspired by the swinging arches of stone to create similarly noble and dynamic designs in sound. But there is much more in Bach's music than this. His compositions are the crown and the glory of the polyphonic masterpieces of the great Italian and German composers of the seventeenth century, such as Frescobaldi and Schütz, Buxtehude and Froberger, who were all inspired by strong religious feeling. It is this same quality of deep feeling in much of Bach's music that grips us and grows on us the more we hear it.

Moderato

Subject of Fugue from Prelude and Fugue in A minor for organ

LISTEN TO SOME OF THESE RECORDS

Sumer is icumen in. Alleluia Psallat. *Dunstable:* Quam pulchra es. *Palestrina:* Missa brevis (Agnus Dei 2). *Lassus:* Scio enim - Motet. *Tallis:* Adesto nunc propitius - Motet; Lamentations of Jeremiah the Prophet. *Byrd:* Haec dies. *Orlando Gibbons:* The Silver Swan - Madrigal. *Giles Farnaby:* His Toye, *etc. (played on virginals by R. Thurston Dart).* Pelham Humfrey: Hear O Heavens. *Purcell:* Dido's Lament; Suite in D minor *(Harpsichord). Handel:* Israel in Egypt; Organ Concerto No. 4 in F, Op. 4 No. 4. *Couperin:* La Favorite, Rondeau *(Harpsichord). Monteverdi:* May sweet oblivion lull thee *from* The Coronation of Poppaea. *J. S. Bach:* Brandenburg Concertos; Suite in D minor for cello solo *(played by Casals). And any other works mentioned in this chapter.*

CHAPTER SIX

Composition Lesson

Author: Hallo, Jonathan. How did you get on with Chapter Five?

Jonathan: Er ... All right. Er ... But it was a bit muddling.

A.: What was?

J.: Er—some of the words.

A.: Which words?

J.: Well, there was something on the last page. (*Looks it up.*) Here it is: "dynamic designs". How can a design be loud and soft?

A.: Yes—it *is* muddling, I agree. But the word "dynamic" has nothing to do with "dynamics" in music. Do you know what a dynamo is?

J.: Of course, a machine.

A.: What kind of machine? What does it do?

J.: It makes energy—to drive things with.

A.: Just so. And you might say that some music is full of energy or drive. Did you listen to the *Brandenburg Concerto* on the radio yesterday afternoon?

J.: Yes, I did. It was smashing! I think I can see what you mean. But what makes the drive in the music?

A.: It's partly the sense of moving on —or growing. It's also something like the way the arches in a church follow one another. You can see it in the picture on p. 49.

J. (*Looks it up*): Yes, I see. But what has this got to do with music?

A.: Quite a lot. Do you remember in the first chapter how we found out that a song is made up of a number of short tunes?

J. (*Thinks*): Yes, I remember.

A.: Couldn't you say, just as well, that each of the short tunes pushes on to the next, one after the other, until you feel that the song is finished?

J. (*Thinks*): Well, yes, I suppose so.

A.: Do you remember what composition is in music?

J.: Y-yes, I think so—something about making a satisfying whole.

A.: That's right. Would you like to do some composition?

J.: Well—yes—but—I'm afraid it's very hard, isn't it?

A.: Not if we do it together. Supposing we try.

J.: All right. Let's have a go!

A.: Do you remember what a rhythmic pattern is?

J.: Oh yes. I tried clapping some different songs and asking people to guess what they were.

A.: And did they guess?

J.: Not always. But they did guess the easy ones.

A.: Good. Now supposing you invent a rhythmic pattern. Just clap anything that comes into your head.

J. (*Thinks, claps hesitantly, thinks*): I can't think of anything.

A.: Never mind. What's your name?

J.: Jonathan.

A.: I mean your full name.

J.: Jonathan Clarkson.

A.: How old are you?

J.: I'm ten and a half.

A.: All right. Now say your full name again, but this time add the words "ten and a half".

J.: Jonathan Clarkson, ten and a half.

A.: Good. Now say it again, this time clapping as well. Again. Good. Now clap the rhythm without saying anything.

J. (*Starts, hesitates, stops*): D'you mean me to clap (*clapping*) "one, two, three, four"?

A. (*Laughs*): No. Sorry. That's one of the muddling things about the names we use in music. "Rhythm" can mean a good many different things. When we talk about clapping or tapping the "rhythm" of a piece of music, we usually mean the rhythmic pattern. Now clap your rhythm.

J.: Well, but—what would you say if you wanted me to clap the—er—pulses?

A.: Jolly good question. I should probably say: clap in time with the music.

J.: I see. Shall I clap the rhythm now?

A.: Yes, please.

J. (*Claps*): Da-da-der der der.

A.: Weren't you going to add "ten and a half"?

J.: Oh, yes. I forgot. (*Claps.*)

A.: Good. Clap it again. Thank you. Do you think you could write that rhythm down?

J.: Yes, I think so. (*Claps, then writes.*)

A.: How would you beat time to it? Where do you think *"one"* comes?

J. (*Beats and sings*): Da-da-der der der, *der* da-da der.

A.: Good. So where will the bar lines come?

J.: Here and here (*writing them in*).

A.: Fine. And you remember, you don't need to write a bar line at the beginning of the line. What about a time signature? What would it be? Write it in.

J. (*Writing*): Four-four. Isn't that common time?

A.: Quite right.

J.: Then I can write a capital C instead of four-four, can't I?

A.: Certainly.

J.: Can I have the rubber? Thank you. (*Writes.*)

A.: Good. Now tap your rhythm over and over again on the little table. That's right. Go on tapping it and see if a tune comes into your head.

J. (*Taps for a little while*): I can't think of anything to sing.

A.: Can't you? Never mind. Let's try something different now. (*Thinks.*) Did you understand the bit about recitative in Chapter Five?

J.: Oh yes. I sang everything instead of speaking, for a bit, and then the family told me to shut up.

A.: And did you write any of it down?

J.: Well—no—actually. I meant to at first, but then I forgot—sorry.

A.: It doesn't matter at all. Let's try some now. First say your name again.

J.: With the ten and a half bit as well?

A.: Certainly.

J. (*Gabbling*): JonathanClarksontenandahalf.

A. (*Laughs*): Now say it again, a bit slower, and notice where your voice goes up and down. Say it twice. Good. Now, instead of just saying it, sing it.

J. (*Sings hesitantly*): Jon - a - than Clark . . . (*Stops.*)

A.: Tap the rhythm once or twice, then go on tapping while you sing.

J. (*Taps the rhythm twice, then sings boldy*): Jon-a-than Clark-son ten and a half.

A.: Fine. Do you think you could find the first note on the piano?

J. *After one or two wrong notes, plays the right one.*

A.: What is the name of that note?

J. (*Counting up from middle C*): C, D—it's E!

A.: Can you write it down?

J.: I think so. May I look up the table?

A.: Of course.

J. *Looks it up and writes.*

A.: That's right. Now sing your tune again. Good. What comes next?

J. (*Sings*): Der-der der. May I find it on the piano?

A.: Certainly.

J. *Plays E F G.*

A.: Write them down with the right rhythm. Look, here, under the notes you wrote before. Good, What's the next note? Does it go up or down?

J.: Up.

A.: Is your tune a scale tune or a chord tune?

J. (*Thinks*): It starts with a scale tune, but then it changes. May I play it? (*Plays as far as A; thinks.*) I don't know.

A.: Could it be part of a chord tune?

J.: Yes. I think the next note is F.

A.: Would you like to make sure at the piano?

J. (*Plays*): Oh, it's wrong!

A.: Should it be higher or lower? Try again.

J.: All right. (*Plays E.*) (*Delightedly*) Yes. It's right! It's E.

A.: Good. Write it in. What's that interval? Do you remember?

J. (*Counts down*): It's a fourth.

A.: Very good. What comes next?

J. (*Sings*): It goes up again.

A.: What interval?

J. (*Counts on piano*): It's G—that's a third up.

A.: And after that?

J. (*Sings*): Just down one and back again.

A.: What notes, then?

J. (*Plays*) G F G.

A.: Write them.

J. *Writes.*

A.: And then?

J. (*Sings*): Another jump.

A.: What interval?

J. (*Sings and thinks*): Is it another fourth?

A.: Yes, well done. So what note is it?

J. (*Counts down*): D. (*Writes.*) May I sing it now?

A.: Yes. Do.

J. (*Sings*): What do I do next?

A.: Better put in the phrase mark.

J.: Oh, have I written a phrase?

A.: What do you think?

J.: Well—I suppose I have. (*Sings it softly, putting in the phrase mark.*)

A.: What are you going to do now?

J. (*Thinks, then hums quietly twice*): Could I have it twice?

A.: Why not? Write it down. Good.

Well, how would you like to go on?

J.: Er—well—yes—but—this is where it gets hard, isn't it?

A.: Not really. This is where it begins to get interesting. Composing is like building. You have to make a plan first.

J.: How can I make a plan?

A.: You could think of some songs you know where the first phrase is repeated, and see how many phrases there are and how they are planned.

J. (*Thinks a little*): May I look up the book?

A.: Certainly.

J.: ... The first phrase is repeated in *All through the night*.

A.: So it is. And how many phrases are there altogether?

J. (*Sings and counts*): Four.

A.: All right. You could have four phrases in your piece, with the first two the same. How many bars in each phrase of your piece?

J. (*Looks*): Two.

A.: So how many more bars do you need?

J.: Another four.

A.: All right. Mark out four more bars, going on from the last phrase. Just put the bar lines in and leave enough room for the music.

J.: Here? (*Writes.*) Like this? That's four bars.

A.: Right. Now, how long is your

whole piece going to be?

J.: Won't that do?

A.: Yes, I suppose it would. It depends whether you want to build a small house or a large house.

J.: Yes, it is a bit small. It's really only like one room. I could have another room next to it.

A.: Very good idea. That means how many more bars?

J. (*Counts*): Eight. Shall I mark them out?

A.: Yes, and it might be useful to number them too. And the first eight, so this lot starts from "nine".

J. (*Writes*).

J.: Now what?

A.: Give the music something to go to. I mean, compose the last phrase now.

J.: Ooh, that's a good idea! I'm going to end it with the first phrase, like it does in *All through the night*.

A.: Better sing it before you decide... Does it sound like a good ending?

J. (*Sings; thinks*): No... It's no good for an ending at all.

A.: Why not?

J.: It doesn't end on the home note.

A.: Could you alter it just a little to make it end on the home note? Sing the home note.

J.: *Sings C.*

A.: That's right. Now clap your tune and sing it again, making it end on the home note.

J. (*Sings first bar, hesitates, then ends with*): Pom, pom, pom.

A.: Good. Write it down quickly before you forget it.

J.: *Writes in the last two bars.*

A.: How would you like to lead up to this last phrase?

J.: I don't know. How can I?

A.: Well, you balanced your first phrase by repeating it.

J.: Oh yes. Well, I could balance this one by repeating this.

A.: All right. Sing it twice and see how you like it.

J. (*Sings*): No. It gets to the home note too soon, doesn't it, because the cadence isn't till the last bar?

A.: I quite agree. Try singing the first two bars in that place and see how you like it.

J. (*Sings*): Yes, it fits all right. It

seems to make the last bit even more of an ending.

A.: Good. Now you've got a beginning and an ending. What's the next bit to plan?

J. (*Laughs*): The middle, of course!

A.: Now, where's the very middle of the piece?

J. (*Counts*): Here. Bar eight.

A.: All right. Let's call that halfway house and put a double bar in (see p. 30). Right. If the two halves of your piece are going to balance, each one must have an ending. But, of course, the middle ending must not be as definite as the last one.

J.: How can I do that?

A.: You could make it end on the dominant instead of on the tonic. In fact, a very easy way would be simply to transpose your last phrase into the dominant. Do you think you could do that?

J.: I'll try. The dominant would be G, wouldn't it?

A.: Quite right. Play G, and sing your last phrase with G as the home note.

J. *Plays and sings.*

A.: Good. Write it down in bars seven and eight.

J. *Writes B C D E B D A G.*

A.: Good. Now you've got a beginning and an ending for the first half. How many phrases do you need to fill in?

J. (*Counts*): Only one. This ought to be something different, or else my piece will be the same all through. What shall I do?

A.: Sing what you've got so far, just tapping the two empty bars.

J. (*Sings the first two phrases, clapping; stops*): I can't find the B.

A.: Sing up the scale till you find it.

J. (*Sings four minims, E, F sharp, G and A, then B*): Couldn't I use that for the third phrase?

A.: Good idea. Write it down.

J. *Writes E F G A.*

A.: Play what you've written on the piano.

J. (*Plays*): Oh, the F sounds wrong. Ah, I remember now. It should be F sharp. (*Writes*)

A.: Good. Now sing the first four phrases.

J. *Sings.*

A.: How do you like that?

J.: It's not bad, but the new bit's not very exciting.

A.: You could help it by speeding up the rhythm in bar six.

J.: How?

A.: By dividing the minims into shorter notes.

J.: Oh.... D'you mean like the "divisions" in Chapter Five?

A.: Good for you! So what notes will you have now in bar six?

J.: They'll be crotchets. Shall I have two of each, two G's and two A's?

A.: Good idea. Write them in. Now sing it again.

J. (*Sings*): Yes, that moves on better. I say, we're getting on now—I've only got three more phrases to write!

A.: How will you begin?

J.: I know—I'll have the same phrase as I started with, but beginning on B.

A.: Don't you think that's a bit much? How many times have you got it already?

J. (*Counts*): Twice.

A.: What about the cadence phrases?

J.: They're different, aren't they?

A.: Not really. They only end differently.

J.: Oh—well—yes, I suppose so. (*Thinks.*) Could I start the second half with the new tune?

A.: Do you want to lead up to something again?

J.: No, I want to lead down. (*Thinks.*) Could I make it go the other way?

A.: Certainly. Do you remember what an inversion is?

J.: Er—yes, something in a fugue. But isn't it very difficult?

A.: Well, you've just suggested an inversion yourself.

J.: Have I?

A.: Yes, if you turn a tune upside-down, that's an inversion. (*Pointing to bars five and six.*) Sing this phrase again.

J. *Sings E, F sharp, G G A A to "la".*

A.: Now sing it upside-down.

J.: What note shall I start on?

A.: Where do you want to lead down from?

J.: Where I've just got to. (*Looks it up.*) That's G.

A.: All right. Here it is. (*Plays G.*) Start.

J. (*Points and sings, slowly*): La, la, la la la la. (*G, F, E E D D*). I like that. Can I have it all upside-down?

A.: You'd better ask the composer—he's the only one who can say. Who is the composer of this piece?

J.: Gosh!—It's me! Well—I'm jolly well going to have all that bit upside-down.

A.: Fine. Can you already hear what it all sounds like upside-down?

J.: N-no.

A.: All right. How do you know that's

what you want? Don't look so worried. Take this bit of music paper and work it out; then you can sing it and see if you like it.

J. (*Crestfallen*): Oh, I thought it was going to be easy—just saying, "I'll have this," and it would be all right because I'm the composer. But I've still got to do the hard bits. What shall I do now?

A.: Better write what you've just sung.

J. (*Sings and writes G F E E D D*):

Where do I go after this?

A.: Just notice what you've been doing and go on doing it. Look— at the fifth bar the tune went up four notes, one at a time, and in the inversion you've written four notes down, one at a time. Can you see the last note of the sixth bar?

J. (*Finds it*): Yes. Here.

A.: How many notes up is it to the first note of the seventh bar?

J.: One.

A.: Good—so how many notes down will your next note be in the inversion?

J.: One, of course. Oh, I see—I just have to do the opposite. (*Writes with much counting of intervals.*) Is this right?

A.: Very good. Only one mistake. You have made the last note go down instead of up. What should it be?

J.: Oh, yes. E, of course.

A.: Right. Now sing the whole inversion.

J. (*Sings, then stops*): It's a bit jumpy. Could I use the piano?

A.: Certainly.

J. (*Plays and sings*): Yes. I do like it. I'm going to write it in. (*Writes.*)

A.: Fine. Now sing the whole piece.

J. *Sings rather slowly and hesitantly.*

A.: Is this supposed to be a jolly piece or a sad piece?

J.: A jolly piece, of course.

A.: Then what about its tempo— should it be fast or slow?

J.: Fast.

A.: Do you know the Italian word for that? No? It's Allegro. (*Spells.*) ...Right. Now what about the dynamics?

J.: Well, that's sort of medium.

A.: Do you mean fairly loud or fairly soft?

J.: Fairly loud.

A.: Do you remember how that's written?

J.: Yes. (*Writes **mf**.*) Can I sing it now?

A.: Yes, do.

J. *Sings.*

A.: Well, how do you like it?

J.: I like it all right, but it sounds a bit samey.

A.: Go through it again in your head and tell me where the climax is.

J. (*Thinks*): Here. Bars seven and eight.

A.: Do you want the climax loud or soft?

J.: Loud, of course. So I put *f* here.

A.: Good. Do you want it suddenly loud?

J.: No. I want to build up to the climax. I know, I could use a hair-pin.

A.: Very good. How does the second half begin—loud or soft?

J.: I'd like the first phrase soft and the next one getting louder.

A.: Then what should you write?

J.: First a *p* and then a *crescendo*—I mean, another hairpin.

A.: And the last two phrases?

J.: I'll have those medium again, *mf*

A.: Good. Have you got all the phrase marks in? And a double bar at the end?

J.: No, I forgot. (*Writes.*)

A.: Fine. Now sing it right through, in the right tempo and with the right dynamics. Oh, and by the way, wouldn't you like to repeat each half?

J.: What for?

A.: Well, it's often done in short pieces. Like the Court dances, do you remember? (see p. 42).

J.: . . . Yes, minuets and things. Were they repeated? Well, all right. Does that mean I've got to write it all over again?

A.: Oh, no. There's a useful sign for repeats. Just dots near the double bars. Here and here and here.

J. *Writes.*

A.: Good. And at the beginning.

J.: Should I put dots there too? Where?

A.: Just here. Now sing the whole piece, but beat a bar first.

J. *Beats and sings.*

A.: Well, how do you like it?

J.: It's not bad. Can I give it a name?

A.: Certainly. What would you like to call it?

J.: I'd like to call it a jolly piece, but it seems a bit silly.

A.: Not at all. But if you like you can give it an Italian name. A jolly piece in Italian would be *Pezzo Giocoso* (*Pets*-so-jo-*ko*-so).

J.: I like that! How do you spell it? Where shall I write it?

A.: Here, in the middle of the page.

J.: *Pezzo Giocoso*—a jolly piece. (*Thinks.*) I wish I could make it sound a bit jollier.

A.: You can.

J.: How?

A.: By phrasing it.

J. (*Surprised*): But I have put the phrasing in!

A.: Ah, yes. You've marked out the phrases. But phrasing has another meaning, too. You can show how you want the piece sung or played.

J.: What do you mean?

A.: Well, look here. (*Pointing*) If you want these notes *legato*—that means joined together—you can join them with a slur, like this. If you want them *staccato*—that means short—you can put dots over or under them, like this.

J.: Oh, I see. Let me try. (*Sings and writes.*) Will this do?

A.: Very good. Now the second phrase is the same. What are you going to do for the third?

J.: I don't know.

A.: Well, you wanted to make it sound a bit jollier. Sing it in a jolly way and see what happens.

J. (*Sings very energetically.*)

A.: Very good. Did you notice what you did?

J.: Oh—I'm not sure. I think I started with it smooth and then joined up some of the crotchets.

A.: Splendid. So you did. Now put the marks in. That's right. . . No, you sang the last note in bar ten staccato.

J.: Can I have the rubber, please? Thank you. What did I do in bars eleven and twelve? Oh, I remember. I did all the crotchets staccato.

A.: Yes, that's right. Now sing the rest of the piece and put the phrasing in. Good. Now sing it again.

J. *Sings, writes, rubs out, writes, sings.*

A. Do you think it sounds jollier now?

J.: Oh yes. Much more like a jolly piece. . . . Could it be played on a recorder?

A.: I'm afraid it goes too low for a recorder. (*Thinks and looks through the manuscript.*) But it would be all right if you altered bars eleven and twelve.

J.: Would it? Let me try. (*Looks and thinks and hums*). I could make bars eleven and twelve a sequence of bars nine and ten, couldn't I?

A.: Good idea. What note will you start on?

J. (*Sings several phrases, then decides*): I could start on A. Shall I write it here? (*Rubs and writes.*)

A.: Yes. That's right. And don't forget the phrasing. Slurs and dots. Good. But if it's for recorder you will need to take a breath somewhere. What about putting a rest here instead of a note? Sing from bar nine again.

J. (*Sings*): Yes, it does make it better. (*Rubs and writes.*)

A.: Would you like to sing the whole piece now?

J. *Sings.*

A.: How do you like it now?

J.: Much better. Can I put my name on it?

A.: Certainly. Over here, on the right. And under the title put "for recorder".

J. (*Writing*): *Pezzo Giocoso* for recorder, by Jonathan Clarkson.

Hooray! Now I feel like a real composer!

CHAPTER SEVEN

The Age of the Sonata

A. AND D. SCARLATTI, THE EARLY SONATA · C. P. E. BACH
AND SONATA FORM · HAYDN AND MOZART · BEETHOVEN ·
SCHUBERT

SONATA MEANS music for playing, but the name is generally used for a certain type of composition for one or two instruments.

The Italian name "sonata", however, was also used for other kinds of instrumental compositions (such as Purcell's *Golden Sonata* on p. 39). Two of these types of sonata are found in the compositions of a remarkable father and his remarkable son, Alessandro and Domenico Scarlatti, the most famous members of an Italian family of musicians.

Alessandro Scarlatti was chiefly a composer of operas and cantatas, some of which are still performed today; but he also wrote many "sonatas" for four stringed instruments, two violins, viola and cello, and he may thus be regarded as the inventor of the *string quartet*.

Domenico Scarlatti (who, by the way, was born in the same memorable year as Bach and Handel, 1685) launched out in a speciality of his own: short compositions, called sona-

tas, for the harpsichord. He wrote over five hundred of these, most of them lively and witty and very difficult, for he was a brilliant harpsichordist. (They go very well on the modern piano, and concert pianists sometimes include them in their programmes.) All these sonatas consist of single movements in two sections, each of which is repeated. Here is the theme of one of his best-known sonatas, in C major:

Domenico Scarlatti (1685-1737): Sonata in C
(Longo 104)

Every one of these hundreds of sonatas by Domenico Scarlatti grows out of its own individual seed into its own individual shape. But all their adventures may be summed up like this:

they set out from a home key, they explore a number of other keys, and then they find a way back to their home key again.

In Germany, a generation later, another son of a great father made some interesting experiments. This was C. P. E. Bach, usually known as Emanuel Bach, one of the most famous sons of John Sebastian Bach.

Emanuel Bach was a splendid harpsichord player, and he wrote some brilliant keyboard music. But he was not satisfied with this for long, for he said that the purpose of music was "to move the heart". By combining a number of different features of the music of his time, he extended the existing sonata into something more dramatic, more capable of expressing different kinds of feelings. His sonatas contained three contrasting movements. The first of these was usually a lively piece in what has come to be called *sonata form* or "first movement form". The second movement was generally a slow one in the form of an air, very like a *da capo* aria. The third movement was often in lighter style, bright and brisk, sometimes in *rondo* form, based on the French *rondeau*.

Sonata form (or first movement form) could be described as the adventures of two groups of tunes. It begins with the *exposition*, which, as in the fugue, contains the first entry of all the themes: the *first group* in the home key and the *second group*

generally in the dominant. Usually the whole exposition is repeated.

The next part (of the first movement) is called the *development*. Here any one of the tunes can start off a set of adventures in search of an interesting way back to the home key. This part of the first movement is sometimes the most exciting part of the whole sonata.

Once the home key has been reached, the *recapitulation* begins. Here all the tunes pass before us as they did in the exposition, but now they are all in the home key.

Sometimes there is a tailpiece to these adventures. It is called the *coda* (Italian for tail) and it is generally a final comment on what has gone before.

To give you an idea of the scheme or shape of a first movement in "sonata form", here is Jonathan's piece (from Chapter Six) expanded into sonata form.

EXPOSITION

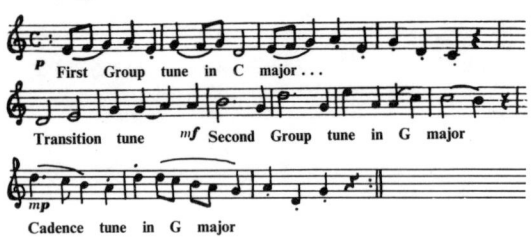

DEVELOPMENT

This could start with an inversion of the First Group tune, combined with the Second Group tune, like this:

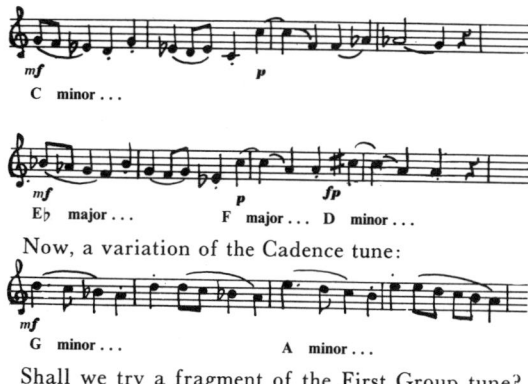

C minor...

Eb major...   F major... D minor...

Now, a variation of the Cadence tune:

G minor...   A minor...

Shall we try a fragment of the First Group tune?

Eb major...   F major... G major...

Having at last reached G and hammered it home, it now feels like a dominant, leading us back to the home key.

RECAPITULATION

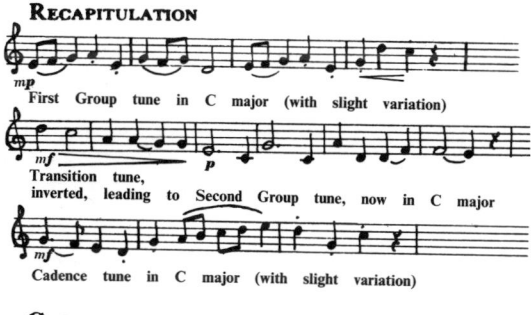

First Group tune in C major (with slight variation)

Transition tune, inverted, leading to Second Group tune, now in C major

Cadence tune in C major (with slight variation)

CODA

Cadence tune in F major   First group tune in C major

The coda often touches the subdominant key; this makes the return to the home key sound more final. The augmentation in the last two bars serves the same purpose.

This is only a tiny model of a sonata form movement, and all it does is to give you a rough idea of the basic structure. There are no two sonatas with exactly the same shape in every detail, just as there are no two fugues with exactly the same shape in every detail. But when you have some idea of the way the music grows, it does help you to share in its adventures.

When listening to a real sonata, try to notice chiefly these things: the moods and characters of the various tunes and the differences between them; the feeling of finality in the cadence tunes; the feeling of drama and tension during the development and the excitement or relief of reaching the home key at the beginning of the recapitulation, when the first tune comes again; the slight variations composers sometimes make in their first-group tunes and second-group tunes during the recapitulation; if there is a coda, notice how it uses the tunes you have been hearing, and how it seems to say "goodbye", firmly or reluctantly, tenderly or humorously, sadly or triumphantly.

Emanuel Bach was a very fine composer, and he wrote some splendid sonatas in the new style. In his lifetime he had a great reputation, and after his death his music was an inspiration to three of the greatest composers of all time: Haydn, Mozart and Beethoven.

We often think of Haydn and Mozart together, but when we compare their lives we find that they are full of contrasts. Haydn was born, and spent his childhood, in a remote Austrian village, where he must often have heard the songs and dances of the Croatian peasants who lived there.

It is sometimes said that Haydn was of Slavonic descent, but in fact he came of a German family. Perhaps the merry tunes that filled his mind, and are never far from his music, were partly remembered from his childhood. His musical training was of the sketchiest kind, and he was largely self-taught. Mozart, on the other hand, was born into a very musical family in Salzburg, a centre of culture in Austria where music played an important part. Young Mozart took to music like a duck to water, and he could play and compose almost before he could read or write. As a musical prodigy, he was acclaimed by kings and queens, but having a father who

was a wise musician, his further training was not neglected. In spite of his phenomenal achievements, young Mozart was always ready to learn more, and to this end he was put in touch with some of the leading musicians of his time.

Later in life the tables were turned. Haydn achieved fame and prosperity in his middle years and lived to a ripe old age, when he was affectionately known as "Papa Haydn". Mozart reached the heights of celebrity in his childhood; as a young man he richly fulfilled the promise of his early youth, and his compositions were recognised as masterpieces. Imagine how terribly hard it must have been for him to find that, with all his work and with all his fame, he could not earn

Mozart as a boy

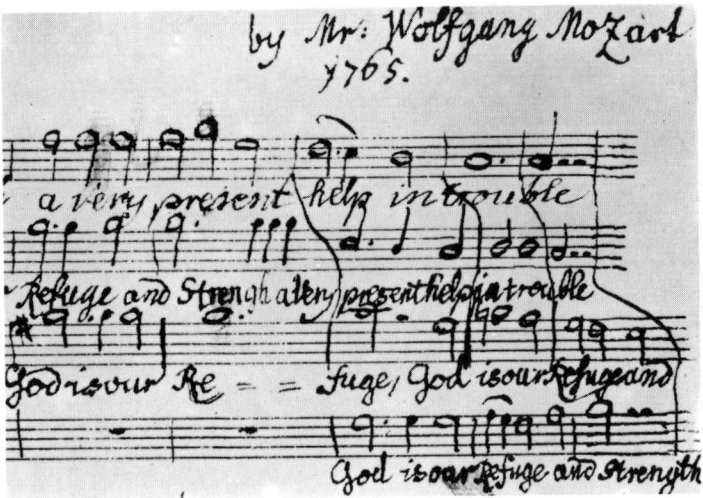

While in London with his family, in 1765, young Mozart composed a motet, God is our Refuge. *Here is part of it, in his own writing and with his own signature*

enough by his composition to live on properly. He died young and in poverty.

Thus Haydn's life overlapped Mozart's. The two masters had the greatest regard for one another, and their mutual admiration resulted in some wonderful music. For instance, Mozart admired some of Haydn's string quartets so much that he was inspired to write six string quartets himself. He sent these to Haydn, who in his turn was so excited by them that he wrote another six string quartets even more beautiful than his earlier ones.

Both Haydn and Mozart were servants of the aristocrats, who used to employ professional musicians in their palaces. As well as providing a musical background to family meals, they had to give regular concerts which were brilliant social occasions. But besides this, some of these aristocrats were genuine music-lovers, who were not content merely to listen, but who also played an instrument themselves. Together with their composer and a couple of the best players from their orchestra, they would retire to a small room to play music in an intimate manner, far removed from the brilliance of the formal concerts in the state rooms of their castles and palaces. This kind of music-making was called *chamber music*.

The rise of chamber and orchestral

Joseph Haydn (1732-1809)

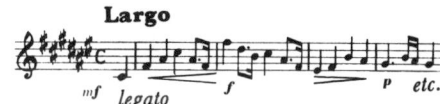

Haydn: Largo from String Quartet in D major *(Op. 76 No. 5)*

Wolfgang Amadeus Mozart (1756-1791)

music is largely due to these noble patrons of the arts, who prided themselves on the size of the orchestras they employed as other aristocrats prided themselves on the size and quality of their stables. Mozart was born into such an environment, his father being the principal violinist employed in the orchestra of the Archbishop of Salzburg. Haydn, after an obscure and poverty-stricken youth, spent over thirty years in the employ of the famous Hungarian Prince Esterházy. Thus he had every opportunity for musical experiment, and he made the most of these opportunities by unifying all the varieties of material at his disposal into a special style of his own. In the course of his long career, he wrote eighty-three string quartets and over a hundred symphonies. Haydn's symphonies have four movements, one of which is usually a *minuet and trio*—that is, a minuet (for full orchestra) of which both sections are repeated (as in the old instrumental dance-suite), followed by another minuet (for fewer instruments) in the same form, after which the first minuet is played again, but without repeats.

Haydn's orchestra consisted mainly of strings—that is, first and second violins, violas, violoncellos (cellos for short) and double basses. In addition, he used a few woodwind instruments, sometimes two flutes, two oboes and two bassoons—sometimes only one of each; of the brass family he used horns and trumpets as available; and last but not least, the timpani, or drums with definite pitch that can be tuned according to the key of the music being played, usually to the notes of the tonic and dominant (or subdominant) (see p. 32).

Some of Haydn's symphonies show his sense of humour. In the slow movement of the *Surprise* Symphony, he gave his audience a shock by putting a loud bang at the end of a very slow and quiet phrase. The *Farewell* Symphony was written when Haydn and his colleagues were impatiently waiting to get back to Vienna one autumn, when Prince Esterházy lingered on and on in the country instead of returning to his town palace, as he usually did at that time of the year. Haydn gave him a musical reminder in this way. He wrote a symphony with a bustling finale, *presto,* which surprisingly ended on the dominant (instead of on the tonic) and then passed on to an extra movement, slow and appealing, beginning as on p. 66.

For a time they all played together, then one by one their parts came to an end. One by one, each player put his instrument down and quietly walked out; until at last only two violins were left, playing this:

and then they walked out too.

The Prince was highly amused at this witty way of reminding him that his musicians wanted to get home. We may be pretty sure that they soon returned to their families, and Haydn too!

About that time a new style of orchestral playing was created in Germany by the Mannheim Orchestra, which not only played magnificently, but which also introduced new and exciting effects. Their crescendo is said to have so excited the audience that they rose in their seats to meet it! Their wide range of dynamics opened up new possibilities of expression for the composers of the time. Mozart, in particular, was much impressed by the Mannheim Orchestra, and its high standard of playing inspired him to write some of his greatest orchestral works, both symphonies and concertos (in which one solo instrument plays the principal part, accompanied by the orchestra).

Apart from his orchestral works, Mozart wrote chamber music, serenades and divertimentos (entertainment music), piano pieces and, above all, operas, which were his lifelong obsession. In one of his letters to his father, he wrote: "... if I only go inside a theatre and hear them tuning up, I am quite beside myself—I am envious of everyone who writes an opera." And no wonder! Mozart's operas are unique in their combination of lovely melody, masterly handling of dramatic situations, the power of bringing to life even the least important of his many characters, irresistible touches of humour, and gaiety that fairly bubbles over. For many music-lovers, *Don Giovanni, The Marriage of Figaro* and *The Magic Flute* are the pick of the operatic repertoire.

Whatever the medium for which he is writing, however gay and lively the mood, one is always reminded sooner or later that the great love of Mozart's musical life was opera. Whether he was writing a string quartet, a symphony or a piano sonata, his melodic line is so vocal, so full of meaning,

Papageno, the comic bird-catcher in The Magic Flute, *prevents the slaves from imprisoning him and Pamina by playing his magic bells and setting them dancing*

that it almost seems to speak. In fact, some of the tunes in his instrumental works are practically the same as tunes in his operas.

Another difference betweeen Haydn and Mozart is in their attitude to the formal conventions of their time. There is rather a contradiction here,

for whereas Haydn spent most of his life outwardly conforming to the behaviour expected of a court composer, in his actual composition he had no qualms about kicking over the traces of formal elegance. Mozart, on the other hand, who could not stand being regarded as a servant, always wrote

Andante

From an aria sung by Pamina *in the second act of* The Magic Flute *when she thinks she has lost her prince for ever . . .*

Adagio

. . . and here is a fragment of melody from the String Quintet in G minor *(K.516). "K" refers to the Köchel catalogue of Mozart's works.*

music that conformed perfectly to the polished tastes and formal elegance of his time. But beneath the formal exterior there was always the singing of a poet; for instance, Mozart often uses the formal background of the so-called Alberti bass; but together with this goes the most expressive melody.

Adagio

From the Piano Sonata in F *(K. 332). *Here Mozart "leans on the wrong notes"; that is to say, he emphasises a melody note which is foreign to the chord*

Finally, there is a subtle difference between the humour of Haydn and the humour of Mozart. In Haydn, the high spirits and sense of fun that prompted him to play pranks in his boyhood stayed with him throughout his life.

Young Haydn cuts off his fellow-choirboy's pigtail - and is dismissed from the choir

In his music this sense of humour expresses itself in jaunty rhythms and unexpected contrasts:

Vivace assai

Haydn: Sonata in F *for violin and piano. Finale*

In Mozart the humour is of a more subtle kind:

Assai allegro

From the Piano Sonata in F *(K. 332). In the second and third bars Mozart anticipates the beats, making an effect of syncopation*

The age of the sonata is dominated by the towering figure of Beethoven, who wrote some of the most powerful music in the world.

Beethoven was born in Germany, where he started his musical career in early youth. At that time Vienna was regarded as the musical centre of Europe—Haydn and Mozart, who lived there, were then at the height of their powers. To Vienna, then, Beethoven was sent when he was seventeen. There Mozart heard him play and improvise, and he was deeply impressed, especially by Beethoven's amazing improvisation. "Watch that young man," he said. "Some day he will make a great noise in the world."

With the insight of genius, Mozart had recognised a brother genius. Here was an artist whose extraordinary music-making not only expressed a fiery and passionate nature, but also revealed an intensely original musical imagination.

While still a young man, Beethoven gradually became deaf. Imagine what a cruel fate this was for a sensitive musician. Small wonder that he became more and more irritable as his deafness increased. As time went on, he became a great trial to his friends, because they never knew what to expect from him—he could be so affectionate and so furious, so gentle and so terrifying by turns.

Even when he could no longer hear any sounds at all, he could imagine musical tones so vividly that he was able to write down all the wonderful music that he heard in his head. Thus, in his art, Beethoven triumphed over his fate. He enriched the world of music by nine great symphonies, as well as by many other great works of every kind.

For Beethoven music always meant something definite. But his music expressed feeling more than it painted pictures—even in his *Pastoral* Symphony, which he himself described as "Memories of Life in the Country". He was usually very rude when somebody asked him what one of his works "meant", but he did tell us in words what some of them were about.

Ludwig van Beethoven (1770-1827)

For instance, he headed the three movements of one of his piano sonatas: *Farewell, Absence, Meeting Again*; in a string quartet he wrote the words: "Must it be? It must be." Once, when asked about the meaning of one of his most dramatic piano sonatas, he gave the mysterious answer: "Read Shakespeare's *Tempest*."

When a poet wants to express a feeling or an idea, he can make either a poem or a drama. Beethoven, the tone-poet, chose drama. "But this is music," you will say. "What has drama to do with it?" Quite a lot. The essence of drama lies in the creation of contrasting characters, the conflict and adventure arising out of their impact on one another, and the resolution of this conflict in tragedy or triumph. This is exactly what happens in a Beethoven sonata.

Beethoven's themes are always clearly defined in character, and often his first-group tunes are in striking contrast to his second-group tunes.

First Group tune from the Piano Concerto in C minor, *Op. 37*

Second Group tune from the same concerto

First Group tune from The "Kreutzer" Sonata *for violin and piano, Op. 47. The "Kreutzer" Sonata (so called because it was dedicated to a violinist of this name) is one of Beethoven's best known sonatas for violin and piano. It opens with a slow introduction, after which the exposition begins with this tune, first given out by the violin and then repeated by the piano*

Second Group tune from the same sonata.

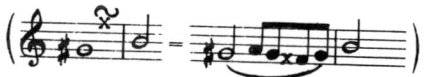

This ornament is called a turn, *and the notes in the bracket show how it should be played.*

When you get to know the exciting development sections in some of his works—for instance, the first movement of the *Appassionata*—you will realise that the drama and tension in them are expressions of Beethoven's own spiritual conflicts and adventures. And when you come to the end of some of his works whose slow movements ask questions to which there seem to be no possible answers—the grief and despair in the *Third Symphony*, the insistent searching in the

Fifth, the reluctant resignation in the *Seventh*—you will feel that, with the utmost certainty and triumph, Beethoven has found real answers to them all.

Beethoven: Seventh Symphony, *slow movement*

Beethoven's stupendous musical imagination demanded infinite varieties of tone colour in order to express exactly what he wanted to express. He revolutionised the orchestra and made unheard-of demands on chamber music players. His writing for the piano, which constantly suggests orchestral colour, went far beyond the limitations of the piano-playing of his time. Though he sometimes wrote easy pieces for the beginner, most of Beethoven's piano works will always remain a challenge to pianists of every kind.

Beethoven wrote one opera, *Fidelio*. In this, as in the choral finale of his *Ninth* Symphony, he voiced his ideals of freedom and brotherhood.

Thus, thanks to these great masters, Haydn, Mozart and Beethoven, Vienna became a treasure-house of classical masterpieces. Widely different though they were, these composers had certain qualities in common. They shared the same ideals: truth of expression and beauty of form; and it was their impulse to fuse these into eloquent musical shapes that inspired them to create their greatest works.

These composers have come to be known as "the Viennese Classics", together with Schubert, who was actually born in Vienna and died there when he was only thirty-one. As with Purcell and Mozart, the most lovely melodies seemed to pour from him without any effort. In fact, Schubert was hard put to it to get his music down on paper fast enough. He would scribble on anything, even on the

Schubert (1797-1828), playing to his friends

backs of restaurant menus. He wrote many sonatas and symphonies as well as chamber music, and some of the most beautiful passages in all music can be found in these works. Perhaps you know the *Unfinished* Symphony. In the second movement there is a solo for the clarinet (later the oboe has it) which shows us how modulation can change the whole meaning of a note in the melody. Schubert's expressive use of modulation is often sheer magic.

The chords in the lower stave indicate the harmonies in the strings. Notice how these harmonies change the meaning of the long notes in the tune. (This kind of modulation, where C sharp major becomes D flat major, is called an enharmonic change)

Some of Schubert's closest friends were poets, and he set hundreds of their poems to music. What a cascade of jewels! There is nothing quite like Schubert's *Lieder* (plural of *Lied* pronounced "leed", German for song). Here we have not only the loveliest of melodies, but also—perhaps chiefly —the perfect expression of every nuance of poetic feeling, crystallised in a few notes. Very often this is done in the piano accompaniments, which vividly set the mood and scene of the whole song. Listen to *Whither,* where the piano part suggests a rippling brook; or to the *Hurdy-gurdy Man,* where the forlorn melody in the right hand and the bleak fifths in the left not only suggest a wintry landscape, but also conjure up the piteous figure of the poor old organ-grinder.

With Beethoven and Schubert we are on the threshhold of the *Romantic* era. Romanticism was a new spirit that spread all over Europe early in the nineteenth century. Writers and artists expressed the people's desires and hopes for a new world—a world of liberty and brotherly love. Music, the most directly emotional of the arts, was an admirable vehicle for the Romantic spirit, and though there are signs of it in earlier composers, it is in Beethoven and Schubert that we first hear it clearly expressed in music.

LISTEN TO SOME OF THESE RECORDS

D. Scarlatti: Sonata in C, Longo 104 *(Harpsichord). C. P. E. Bach: Symphonies or Piano Sonatas. Haydn: String Quartets, Symphonies, etc. Mozart: Piano Concertos, etc. Beethoven: Piano Sonatas, String Quartets, Symphonies. Schubert: Lieder, Symphonies,* String Quartet in A minor. *And any other works mentioned in this chapter.*

73

This is what the conductor looks at. Some conductors memorise the full score, with all its detail, so as to be able to conduct more freely

CHAPTER EIGHT

The Orchestra

THE PLAYERS · THE CONDUCTOR · THE STRINGS · THE
WOODWIND · THE BRASS · PERCUSSION AND HARP ·
EXTRA INSTRUMENTS

THE ORCHESTRA has been the back-bone of concert music for nearly two hundred years. You could think of it as a colossal instrument with infinite possibilities of pitch, timbre and dynamics.

The players in a symphony orches-tra need to be fine artists. Many of them give up careers as soloists in order to play in an orchestra. Theirs is an exacting profession. Besides the concerts, for which they have long and tiring rehearsals, they often have recording and film sessions. They must

The London Philharmonic Orchestra, conducted by Dr. Steinberg, at the Royal Festival Hall, London

Miltiades Caridis, the Musical Director and Conductor-in-Chief of the Philharmonia Hungarica

also spend every available moment practising, so as to keep up their standard as first-class performers.

Conducting is the musician's dream. Just imagine what it feels like to stand before that great, living instrument with your head full of wonderful music, to set it going with a flick of your baton, and then, together with your fellow-artists, to have the thrill of re-creating the ever-changing shapes, colours and moods of the music!

A great conductor has the special gift of communicating his joy in the music to the listeners as well as to the players. But, in addition to having the

Sir Malcolm Sargent discusses a point with his leader

music in his bones, he has to have every one of the tiniest details of the score in his head. Also he has to be realistic and practical and to have a good working knowledge of the way each instrument is played. For instance, if he felt that the music demanded a certain effect on the violins, the conductor could either say, "I want bars forty-three to forty-seven light and crisp, please," or else, "At bars forty-three to forty-seven, please play at the very tip of the bow." Which do you think would more easily produce the desired effect?

Probably a great conductor would combine these methods, confiding to the players his reasons for wanting the effect, as well as suggesting a practical way of getting it. In situations of this kind, the conductor sometimes consults the first violinist, known as the "leader" of the orchestra.

If you look at an orchestra in action, you will see that about two-thirds of the players are holding bows in their hands. This is because the main body of the orchestra consists of the *violin* family, usually known as the strings, which consists of the *violin*, the *viola*, the *violoncello* and the *double-bass*. Though these instruments vary in size, they are all made in more or less the same shape, and they all have four strings of gut or metal stretched tightly along them. They are also all played on the same principles: the pitch is varied by pressing the fingers of the left hand on various parts of the four strings, and the tone is produced by drawing a bow across the strings with the right hand.

The pitch of the strings is different for each instrument of the family. The strings are tuned by turning the pegs to which they are attached.

The bow, which is a light stick of springy wood, has a hank of hairs stretched along it which, when rubbed with rosin, cling to the strings as the bow is drawn across them. In this way, the bow sets the strings vibrating. The bow is drawn across the strings slowly and lightly for soft sounds, swiftly and with more pressure for loud sounds. Sometimes the players put their bows down on the music desks and pluck their strings with their fingers. This effect is called *pizzicato,* or plucking.

Like the strings of the piano, the strings of the violin family are rich in harmonics (see p. 18). By lightly touching a string in certain places, the player can produce various harmonics, which have a tone quality quite different (rather fluty) from the stopped notes, where he presses the string down firmly.

All string players occasionally have to use the mute, a small object with three double prongs, which grips the bridge (that holds the strings up) and softens the sound.

The violin is the smallest and highest-pitched instrument of the family. Its strings are tuned in fifths

upwards from G below middle C—that is, G, D, A, E. In a full symphony orchestra there could be about thirty

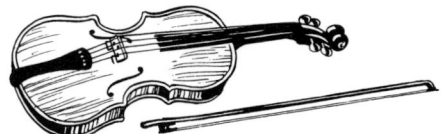

violins, divided into "firsts" and "sesonds". They usually play for most of the time, and they often dominate the music with their melody. Their tone colour is full of variety, and they have a very wide range of pitch —three and a half octaves.

The viola is slightly larger than the violin and its strings are tuned one fifth lower than the violin's. It is played in the same way, but, owing to its "middle of the harmony" pitch and more subdued tone, it rarely has the

principal tune to play. A good opportunity to hear the violas clearly and easily occurs in Bach's *Sixth Brandenburg* Concerto, in which there are no violins—and what a rich and earnest tone the violas have!

When composers use the violas to play the melody, it is usually so as to bring out its sombre or melancholy

On the opposite page, reading from top to bottom on the left *are (1) the violin and the violas (from this section of the orchestra you can see how much larger the violas are than the violin); (2) cellos and (3) double basses.* At the top right *are (4) flutes and a piccolo.* Below them are *(5) oboes and cor anglais, (6) clarinets and bass clarinet, and (7) bassoons and double bassoon.*

On this page *are,* above, *(8) the horn;* on the right, *(9) trumpets, trombones and tuba, (10) harps,* and *(11) part of the percussion section: bass drum, cymbals and side drum; and* below *(12) are the kettledrums*

aspect; in fact, the viola often sounds more at home in a minor key than in a major one.

Tchaikovsky: Sixth Symphony (known as the Pathétique). First movement

The violoncello (or "cello", as it is nearly always called) is much larger than the viola and has to be held the other way round.

Its four strings are tuned in fifths, one octave lower than the viola, so that its top string is the A below middle C. There may be as many as ten or twelve cellos in the orchestra (about the same number as the violas), and they have to work

hard most of the time playing the bass of the harmony—anything from an unbroken line of sound to the lightest *pizzicato*. But occasionally they come into their own when they are used for particularly expressive tunes, when they can produce a wonderfully rich, singing tone.

Schubert: "Unfinished" Symphony. First movement

The double-bass is the largest member of the violin family, and it produces the lowest notes. It is so large that the player has to stand up (or sit on a very tall stool) to play it. It usually has four strings tuned in fourths: E, A, D and G, the highest one (G) being on the bottom line of the bass clef. (Their notes are written an octave higher than they sound.) Most of the time the double-bass plays the same part as the cellos, in unison with them or, more often, an octave lower. They are the foundation of the orchestra, and a symphony orchestra will probably have eight double-basses.

Beethoven: Scherzo (skair-tso) Fifth Symphony. Scherzo, meaning "joke", is the name Beethoven gave to the Minuet movement in his symphonies

80

Next in importance to the strings is the *woodwind* family, consisting chiefly of *flute, oboe, clarinet* and *bassoon.* They all have to be blown, also they are all made of wood (except the flute, which is sometimes made of metal), they usually play in pairs, they all have a wide range of pitch and dynamics, and they are all very agile and equally good at melodious and florid passages.

The sound of the flute varies from

a breathy whisper to a shrill whistle. Its range is high, from middle C to about three octaves above. Here is a typical flute tune:

Dvořák's Fifth *Symphony* ("From the New World") *first movement*

The flute combines well with the oboe. Also it is often used by composers to double (copy) the line of the first violins, to which it lends a silvery edging.

A younger brother of the flute is the *piccolo,* which sounds an octave higher than the flute. Its tone is rather

shrill, and it is, therefore, often used to add brilliance to the *tutti* (when the whole orchestra plays together). Notice it in Bartók's *Concerto for*

Orchestra, however, where it has a haunting duet with the side-drum, suggesting the magic of night.

The range of the oboe is about half an octave less than that of the flute,

and its tone has a nasal, piercing quality, partly due to the double reed through which it is played. Composers often use the oboe for solos, and sometimes to make comments on what other instruments have just played, as, for instance, in the first movement of Beethoven's *Seventh* Symphony, where the oboe seems to say: "This is what the tune really means."

Beethoven: Seventh *Symphony, first movement*

The *cor anglais,* which means "English horn", is neither English nor a horn! It is first cousin to the oboe and

sounds a fifth lower in pitch. It is a transposing instrument—that is to say, it sounds a fifth lower than it plays, so if you want the cor anglais to play middle C you have to write the G above it. The cor anglais has a distinctly plaintive quality. Here is a characteristic melody, as it is written in the score and as it actually sounds:

81

Sibelius. The Swan of Tuonela, *as it is written*

As it actually sounds

The *clarinet* is played through a single reed. It is one of the busiest instruments in the orchestra. It has a very wide range in pitch, from C sharp below middle C for three and a half octaves upwards. It also has an enormous range in timbre and dynamics. No other wind instrument can play as quietly as the clarinet.

The clarinet is a transposing instrument, and a clarinet player has to

have two instruments, one in A and one in B flat, and the composer has to choose the right instrument to suit the music. Here is a short extract from a Mozart symphony which shows the clarinets in two typical aspects, one playing the melody and the other playing the florid accompaniment. This is how it is written in the score, but it will actually sound a tone lower, so that what you hear will be in E flat major, not in F major, as written.

Mozart: Trio from Minuet of Symphony in E flat (K. 543)

The *bassoon,* as you will probably guess from its size, is the lowest in pitch of the woodwind family. It has a double reed, so it is related to the

oboe. It has a special quality of tone when played softly, something like a baritone voice. It can play passages of great agility, especially jumps. Here is a characteristic bassoon part:

Paul Dukas (1865-1935): The Sorcerer's Apprentice

The next family of wind instruments, the *brass,* consists of *horn, trumpet, trombone* and *tuba,* which all have a tremendous range of dynamics. When a composer is building up towards a climax, notice how the brass instruments gradually come in, and how little by little they dominate the orchestra. They are all very difficult to play, partly because their technique is based on a complicated system of overtones; and they are all transposing instruments.

In a full symphony orchestra there are usually four horns (sometimes called "French horns"). They are very

useful instruments, because they blend equally well with either of the other two main families of the orchestra, the strings and the woodwind. They have a wide range, not only of pitch, but also of timbre, and they can issue caressing murmurs as well as threatening roars. A typical passage for horns is the trio of Beethoven's *Eroica* (*Third*) Symphony.

Beethoven: Scherzo, Third *Symphony*

The sound of the trumpet can be the most piercing noise in the orchestra, but the trumpets can also sing most beautifully.

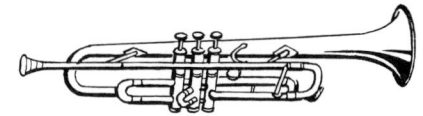

Allegro
Solo trumpet, off stage

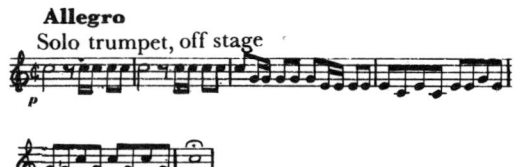

An exciting use of the trumpet occurs in Beethoven's Leonora *Overture No. 3, originally intended for his opera,* Fidelio. *The hero, in prison, hearing this far-off trumpet call, knows that his life is saved*

There are usually two trumpets in the orchestra, but some works demand a good many more.

The trombones—two tenor trombones and one bass trombone—are just that, the tenors and the basses of the brass family. They can make a

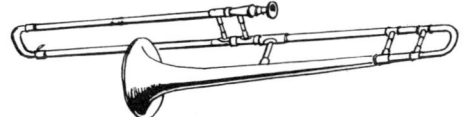

most terrifying blare and a most lovely hush and everything in between. They change the pitch of their basic tones by sliding a part of their instrument in and out—a very familiar sight to the concert-goer, and one which will probably be one of the first things to catch your eye at a symphony concert. Here is a typical trombone passage, solemn and majestic:

Brahms: Fourth *Symphony, Finale*

That great fellow, the tuba, can produce a fearsome roar, but on the whole he limits himself to a role similar to

that of the double-bass in the string family, and he often doubles the part of the bass trombone.

Now we come to the *percussion* family—that is to say, instruments that are not scraped or blown, but hit. Some have definite pitch and some have not. Of those that have definite pitch, the most important are the *kettledrums.*

The kettledrums or, in Italian, the *timpani,* each consist of a metal basin with a parchment stretched across the top, the tension of which is regulated by half a dozen or so taps spaced round the rim. There are three sizes of kettledrums, for low, middle and high

notes; and, adding together the notes available on each one, they have jointly a range of about one and a half octaves, from the G on the top space of the bass clef downwards.

Beethoven: Ninth *Symphony, Scherzo. This is one of the rare occasions where the kettledrums (timpani) appear as a solo instrument, holding their own against the whole orchestra (tutti)*

The kettledrums usually play the bass of the harmony, but as they can play only as many notes as there are drums, they only play at special moments, often at the cadences. They can make exciting effects with the

"drum-roll" (hitting the drums very fast with both sticks alternately), either soft or loud, and especially crescendo or diminuendo. Notice their terrific effect in the passage leading to the finale of Beethoven's *Fifth* Symphony.

However skilful the player is at tuning his drums quickly during a

performance (have you noticed him bending down and almost touching the drum with his ear while he rapidly twists the taps?), he has to take some time over it. But there are nowadays also kettledrums with mechanical tuning (operated by pedals) so that it is possible to make a *glissando* (sliding from one note to another) on the

Tubular Bells

drums. You can hear this effect in Bartók's *Music for Percussion and Strings.*

Other instruments of the percussion group of the symphony orchestra that

Glockenspiel

have definite pitch are the *tubular bells,* the *xylophone,* the *celesta* (used by Tchaikovsky in the *Dance of the Sugar-plum Fairy),* the *Glockenspiel* (used by Mozart in *The Magic Flute)*

and the piano when used as an orchestral instrument by Stravinsky and some other modern composers.

Percussion instruments which have no definite pitch are the *bass drum;* the *cymbals,* which can be either

Bass Drum & Cymbals

clashed together or else struck with a drum-stick, and are equally effective for emphasising a climax or suggesting mystery; the gong, equally good for both these effects; the *side-drum,* very important for military effects—most familiar is its sudden attack and crescendo drum-roll into *God Save the Queen*; and a host of other instruments, such as the following: *anvil,*

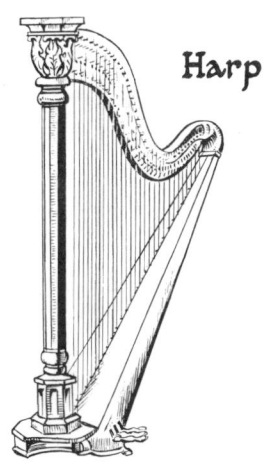

Harp

85

besom, block, castanets, bell, rattle, tambourine, tam-tam, tom-tom, triangle, whistle, wind machine, etc.

The symphony orchestra, especially as used for Romantic music, would be incomplete without at least one *harp.* This has a range almost as wide as the piano. Its strings are plucked by both hands, and their pitch is adjusted by pedals. Its most characteristic sounds are broken chords, *arpeggios* and *glissandos.* It is especially well suited to accompany melodies on the woodwind. Notice it at the end of Debussy's *L'Après-midi d'un faune;* and in Bizet's suite, *L'Arlésienne.*

Besides all the regular instruments of the standard symphony orchestra, there are a good many extras. Bach's trumpet parts are usually played on a special trumpet called a *Bach trumpet.* He also sometimes used an *oboe d'amore.* Mozart sometimes uses a *basset-horn* (a low-pitched clarinet). He also demands *panpipes* for Papa-geno in *The Magic Flute.* Berlioz and Wagner demand many extras: the *E flat clarinet,* the *bass trumpet,* the *cornet,* the *double-bass trombone* and the *Wagner tuba.* Modern composers sometimes use a *bass oboe,* a *heckelphone,* a *bass flute* and *saxophones.*

With the advent of mechanical reproduction, new effects are creeping into the modern orchestra. As far back as the nineteen-twenties, Respighi introduced a gramophone into the orchestra, to play the song of a nightingale in his *Pines of Rome.* Since then still stranger objects have found their way into the symphony orchestra, such as the *vibraphone* and the *marimba,* the *"Ondes Martenot"* (which produce sounds electronically), and even a tape-recorder.

Besides all these, almost anything which makes a noise—from a whip to a typewriter—can be used in the percussion section of the modern symphony orchestra.

LISTEN TO THESE RECORDS

All the works mentioned in this chapter. Also Prokofieff: Peter and the Wolf. *Britten:* Young Person's Guide to the Orchestra.

CHAPTER NINE

The Romantic Century

ROMANTIC MUSIC · THE PIANO AND ITS COMPOSERS ·
THE "MUSIC OF THE FUTURE" · THE CLASSICAL
TRADITION · NATIONALIST COMPOSERS · LATE
ROMANTIC COMPOSERS · DEBUSSY AND RAVEL · OPERA
AND BALLET

ROMANTIC MUSIC, like Romantic poetry, belongs to the world of day-dreams. Here feelings matter more than facts, and the artist's imagination bathes facts and objects in a stream of emotion. When the longed-for new world of freedom and brotherly love failed to materialise, many artists turned away from reality and either created a dream world or else lived in the past. Like Wordsworth's *Solitary Reaper,* Romantic composers sing of "old, unhappy, far-off things and battles long ago".

There is a song by Schubert which hurls us straight into the Romantic era. It is a setting of a poem by Goethe called *Erlking.* There never was such a king on land or sea. A terrified child sees ghostly shapes in the trees which he imagines to be the threatening "Erlking" and his daughters. The father, infected by the child's terror, desperately gallops home, only to find the child dead in his arms.

Here is the opening of the piano part. It goes at a tearing pace and is very difficult to play. Those hammering octaves—or hammering hooves—persist throughout the song with terrifying effect. Try to listen to this song on a gramophone record, and you will hear how vividly it conveys the feelings of the characters in the story.

Schubert: Erlking

With Schubert opening the gate to the Romantic era, a host of composers passes before us whose chief reason for composing was that they wanted to express their personal feelings. It is hardly to be wondered at that much of their music was written for the piano. The piano is a wonderful confidant, for it has the full range of the orchestra in pitch and a wide range of dynamics; it can sing, and with the sustaining pedal it can blend tones in a most fascinating way. A composer might well be more inclined to impart his innermost secrets to the piano than to any other instrument or combination of instruments. Certainly it was so with most of the great composers of the Romantic era.

The German composer Schumann started them off with some delightful pieces for and about children. If you play the piano at all, you probably know some of them. Schumann was a master of the miniature, and even in his shortest and simplest pieces he vividly conveys a mood. Have you ever heard this one? It is called *First Loss,* and you can see even from these few

Robert Schumann (1810-1856)

bars how this music droops with sadness.

Schumann: First Loss *from* Album for the Young

He wrote many concert pieces too. His wife, Clara Schumann, was a famous pianist, and he composed some fine works for the piano which she played all over Europe. Perhaps the best known of these is *Carnaval,* a set of short pieces, each one a miniature-portrait in music: of himself, his wife and some of their friends.

Schumann was a writer as well as a composer. He founded and ran a magazine in which he wrote some splendid articles on music. Among them was one with the title, "Hats off, Gentlemen—a Genius!" It was about Chopin, the gifted young Polish pianist-composer, who was living in Paris. Schumann also wrote of Chopin as "the poet of the piano"; but when we consider the music of both these composers side by side, it is very difficult to decide whether Chopin or Schumann had more right to such a title.

Chopin wrote practically all his music for the piano, and he created an unmistakable pianistic idiom of his own, full of enchanting melodies and most subtle harmonies. His favourite composers were Bach, from whom he learnt how to weave his exquisite contrapuntal textures, and Mozart, with whom he has many qualities in common. Like Mozart, Chopin always sings; and, like Mozart, Chopin achieves the subtlety of his harmonies by leaning on "wrong" (that is, *chromatic*) notes. Like Mozart, too, in Chopin's works the poetic feeling and the musical design are of equal importance. But whereas Mozart's music is expressive even when he sets out to write, say, a formal minuet, Chopin's music is perfectly balanced even when he is moved by a romantic impulse to write a very sad piece, like the *Pre-*

Chopin: Prelude in E minor, *Op. 28 No. 4*

lude above. By the way, if you look at the last music example again, you may notice how differently Schumann and Chopin express sadness in these pieces. With Schumann's *First Loss,*

Chopin playing to his friends

Frédéric Chopin (1810-1849)

Fingal's Cave, visited by Mendelssohn in 1829, inspired him to write his well-known overture The Hebrides

it is all in the shape of the melody; with Chopin, the melody hardly moves, and the expression is all in the harmony.

Mendelssohn and Liszt might also be regarded as poets of the piano, although they wrote much music of other kinds. Mendelssohn's contribution to piano music consists chiefly of

Final bars of overture The Hebrides, *by Felix Mendelssohn-Bartholdy (1809-1847)*

the *Songs without Words,* short pieces in which he expressed a passing mood or impression in a special and unmistakable style of his own. Mendelssohn, born in Germany, was a child prodigy. He reached the height of his powers as a composer at the age of seventeen, with his incidental music to *A Midsummer Night's Dream.* He never wrote anything more beautiful, more apt or more polished than this music, though he later further enriched the concert world with lovely things like the *Hebrides* overture and the *Violin Concerto.* Mendelssohn had a brilliant career, but, like Chopin and Schumann, his life was cut off before he had fairly reached middle age.

Liszt, born in Hungary about the same time as these three tone-poets, lived on to a grand old age. In a way, he was the central figure of the Romantic movement in music. He was the greatest pianist of his time. He, too, had been a child prodigy, and his brilliant career may be said to have been launched at the age of eleven, when his astonishing playing was acclaimed in public by Beethoven, who kissed him before a Viennese audience. As a young man, Liszt was much impressed by the almost legendary figure of Paganini. This Italian wizard of the violin so charmed and bewitched his audiences all over Europe, by his highly original and intensely expressive playing, that swooning ladies had to be carried out

Franz Liszt (1811-1886), at the age of thirteen

piano-playing, the composers to benefit from his unequalled insight, appreciation and encouragement. He enlarged the pianists' repertoire by a great number of piano pieces, most of which demand what is known as "transcendental technique" (a phrase coined by him). In the field of orchestral composition he invented a form known as the "symphonic poem", a work in one movement that was inspired by some picture or story and which had a specific title (Dukas' *The Sorcerer's Apprentice* is a good example). Liszt's own symphonic poems are not often played nowadays, but he started a fashion that lasted for nearly a hundred years.

A composer who was closely associated with Liszt was Berlioz, the great French Romantic composer, and one of the most interesting characters in musical history. To find expression for his intense feelings and grandiose conceptions, none of the existing orchestras or choirs was big enough for him, and he mustered unheard-of numbers of singers and players. Once, during his travels abroad, Berlioz was asked by the King of Prussia if it were true that he demanded five hundred musicians for some of his compositions. He answered: "Sometimes only four hundred and fifty."

of the hall. Liszt admired him so much that he produced equally sensational effects from the piano, drawing frenzied applause from his excited audiences.

Liszt was, however, much more than a superlative pianist. In his compositions, his far-reaching imagination enabled him to create new means of expression which influenced several generations of composers. Added to this, his wide culture and kindly nature helped to make him a valuable figure in the musical life of his day. For many decades pianists and composers flocked to Liszt from all over the world—the pianists to learn about

It was largely thanks to Berlioz' investigations and innovations that the classical orchestra was transformed into the modern one. Taking up the fascinating subject of orchestral colour where Beethoven left off, Berlioz vastly extended the possibilities of orchestral timbre by introducing old and new instruments into the orchestra, by his new combinations of tone colour, and by his special understanding of the way each instrument was played. His music is highly original, not only in its orchestral effects, but also in its melodic material. There is no symphony orchestra of repute that does not include the *Fantastic Symphony* by Berlioz in its repertoire.

Berlioz (1803-1869): Symphonie Fantastique

Another great composer of the Romantic era, contemporary with Berlioz and Liszt and closely associated with them, was Wagner. Berlioz, Liszt and Wagner together represented what they called "The Music of the Future". History has proved them right, in a sense, for Berlioz extended the classical orchestra to its modern proportions, Liszt first began to break the bounds of classical harmony, and Wagner, having at first followed Weber, who had helped to establish German opera with his operas based on old German legends, eventually broke away from all existing traditions and created what he called the "music drama".

Wagner wanted to create every-thing, to have everything, to control everything. His music dramas had to unite all the arts. Even the theatre had to be specially built (the famous Bayreuth Opera House) and, most important of all, a special public had to be created. In order to get the most out of Wagner's music, people had to become part of this special public. They had to think and feel what the composer dictated.

Wagner (1813-1883): Ride of the Valkyries

In most of his works, Wagner made use of the *Leitmotiv* (*lite*-moh-teef), a special type of theme or tune which was used in this way: each character in the story had a special set of tunes, so that when one of them walked on to the stage, the orchestra showed, by playing the right *Leitmotiv,* who he was and what he was feeling. Apart from all this, Wagner was a superb music-maker. He enormously extended the range of orchestral colour, and he created exciting new effects by his use of chromatic harmony. Like Chopin, he leaned on "wrong" notes, and, like him, instead of following a discord by a concord, he followed one

Wagner: Prelude to Tristan and Isolde

discord by another (see p. 16). But Wagner went so far in this that sometimes the sense of key was almost lost.

The novelty of Wagner's chromatic harmony lies chiefly in his continuous use of it for long stretches without cadences definite enough to establish

Johannes Brahms (1833-1897) was born in Hamburg and spent most of his life in Vienna

a key. His name for this continuous flow was "endless melody".

Enthusiasm for the music of the future, and especially for the music of Wagner, rose to feverish heights. But the cult of Wagner did not draw all musicians and music-lovers to its ranks. There was one composer at least who stood aside from the cult of the colossal as represented by Berlioz, Liszt and Wagner, and that was Brahms. Deeply aware of the greatness of Bach, Mozart, Beethoven and Schubert, he turned his back on what seemed to him the shallow fashions of his time, and following in the footsteps of those great master-builders,

Brahms: Third *Symphony, Finale*

he forged a new language of his own in which he wrote some magnificent sonatas, concertos, symphonies and chamber music. But, though he wears the cloak of a Classical composer, he is at heart a Romantic. The feeling of nostalgia—a kind of regret or homesickness for things past and gone, characteristic of many Romantic composers—colours much of Brahms's poetic feeling. This is expressed most intimately in some of his shorter piano pieces, as well as in his songs, some of which are so beautiful that they rank with the finest *Lieder* of Schubert and Schumann.

In a way, the Belgian composer César Franck had many things in common with Brahms. Like him, Franck led a secluded life, devoted entirely to his art. For most of his life he was a church organist in Paris, where he gathered about him a few pupils (including Paul Dukas) who revered the Classical masters as he did. While Franck admired the music of Liszt and Wagner, and even used some of their new ideas of chromatic harmony in his own compositions, their grandiose undertakings were foreign to his nature. Together with Saint-Saëns, Fauré and others, Franck upheld and fostered the Classical tradition in France, and quietly produced some beautiful works such as the *Sonata for Violin and Piano,* the *Symphony in D minor* and the *Symphonic Variations* for piano and orchestra.

César Franck (1822-1890): last movement of Sonata for violin and piano. *(Note that the violin is in canon with the piano)*

A feature of the Romantic century is the rise of national feeling in music. Chopin, in his mazurkas and polonaises, introduced the characteristic rhythms of Polish folk-music. His example was followed by later composers, such as Dvorák, who not only incorporated many of his native Slavonic rhythms and tunes into his music, but also crossed the Atlantic and used native American Negro melodies and rhythms in his famous *New World* Symphony. Grieg, the Norwegian, based many of his delightful compositions on the characteristic melodies and rhythms of his homeland. In Russia, a group of composers including Borodin, Mussorgsky and Rimsky-Korsakov, was fired with the idea of creating a Russian national music. Certainly they all produced lively and colourful music, but perhaps Mussorgsky best succeeded in creating an individual idiom in his operas, his songs about children, and one well-known work for the piano, *Pictures from an Exhibition.*

Mussorgsky (1839-1881): "Promenade" from Pictures from an Exhibition. *(This work is sometimes heard in a masterly orchestral arrangement by Ravel)*

Tchaikovsky, though not a member of the "nationalist" group, and though he composed in a cosmopolitan style, nevertheless betrays an essentially Russian character in his music. His chief medium was the orchestra, and he wrote symphonies and concertos that are among the most popular works in the orchestral repertoire. He is perhaps best known for his ballet music, such as *Swan Lake* and *The Nutcracker Suite;* but he also wrote some fine operas.

Edvard Grieg (1843-1907)   *Peter Ilyitch Tchaikovsky (1840-1893)*

A composer who learnt much from Tchaikovsky, but who stands alone in his highly individual symphonic achievements, is Sibelius. This rugged Finn, the pride of his people, gave us vivid impressions of their homeland in his numerous orchestral works. These include seven symphonies, as well as a number of symphonic works based on ancient Finnish legends.

Allegro

etc.

Sibelius (1865-1957): Tone poem En Saga

In many ways Rachmaninov resembles Tchaikovsky, for he too wrote in a cosmopolitan style, and his music expresses his feelings in typically Russian ways. Another outstanding Russian composer of the late Romantic era was Scriabin. He had many strange beliefs and ideas (as can be seen from the titles of his orchestral works, such as *Poem of Ecstasy, Poem of Fire,* etc.), and he tried to invent a new kind of harmony with which to express them. Turning away from both Classical and Romantic harmony, he tried to create a whole new harmonic language by making up chords out of the intervals of fourths instead of thirds, like this:

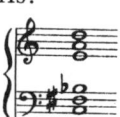

The effect was strange and new, because this kind of harmony weakened the sense of tonality. If you hear any of Scriabin's music you will find that most of it is in pairs of short phrases; nevertheless, it all sounds rather vague, because you can't easily find the home note.

95

Composers in Germany and Austria followed in Wagner's footsteps. Hugo Wolf's fame rests almost entirely on about a hundred songs which have the most striking and original piano parts. The characteristic feature of his music is its frequent changes of key, which follow one another so swiftly that the sense of the basic key is almost lost. The music of Mahler, who wrote ten symphonies, is full of a most haunting nostalgia. This is especially moving in his set of songs with orchestra called *The Song of the Earth.*

Richard Strauss, taking up Liszt's invention of the symphonic tone poem, and further extending Wagner's orchestra, wrote a number of orchestral pieces, such as *Don Quixote* and *Till Eulenspiegel's Merry Pranks,* which are often played at concerts. He also wrote some exciting operas and a few lovely songs.

Towards the end of the Romantic century, musical England stirred in its long sleep and began to make its presence felt in Europe. Since about the time of the death of Handel, England had been regarded on the Continent as "the land without music", even though there were many English music-lovers, and foreign music and musicians were greatly appreciated by them. But it was so long since there had been any great English composers that they were almost forgotten. Now there emerged two distinguished composers, Elgar and Delius. Elgar first made his mark abroad by the beautiful *Enigma Variations* for orchestra. In this work, as in Schumann's *Carnaval,* the variations are tone-portraits of the composer, his wife and his friends. In this, as in his two symphonies and a long tone poem called *Falstaff,* we can admire and enjoy the delicacy of his orchestration as well as the big-sounding tunes and the English fla-

Edward Elgar (1857-1934)

Elgar: "Nimrod" *from the* Enigma Variations

vour of his music. Delius expressed his original genius by the delicacy of his harmonies and the lyrical intensity of his melodies. His orchestral piece, *On Hearing the First Cuckoo in Spring,* is a magical piece of tone painting.

Delius (1862-1934): On Hearing the First Cuckoo in Spring. *Perhaps you can get someone to play this on the piano while you sing the top line. (Or you might manage to play and sing it yourself.)*

A French composer who may be said to have started a new era in music was Debussy. He is sometimes labelled

Claude Achille Debussy (1862-1918)

an "Impressionist" composer, because in some of his music he captured and suggested impressions of Nature, as the so-called Impressionist painters did in their pictures. But, for Debussy, Impressionism was only a point of departure. He was fascinated by beautiful sounds in themselves, which he exploited both in his new use of the orchestra and in his new ways of using traditional harmony. He did this in various ways. First, he went back to some of the earliest tone combinations of musical history. Do you remember the effect of the organum (see p. 24)? Here it is as it appears in Debussy's piano piece, *The Submerged Cathedral,* described in Chapter One, as a series of solid blocks of chords.

97

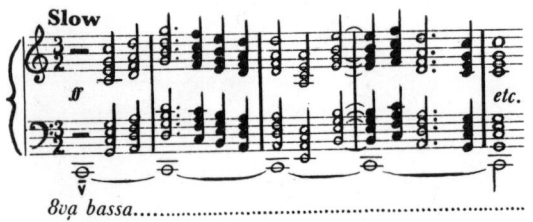

Debussy: The Submerged Cathedral

He also used strange scales based on the medieval church modes (see p. 32) in many of his melodies. Here is an example:

Debussy: Sirènes *(Sirens from Greek mythology) an orchestral piece in which women' voices sing music like this, with eerie effect*

A characteristic feature of Debussy's idiom is his use of the whole-tone scale. There is an orchestral work by him called *Gigues*, in which he uses a well known English folk-tune, *The Keel Row.*

This is what Debussy does with it:

Debussy: Gigues

Can you hear what he has done? He has used the whole-tone scale, so called because there is an interval of a whole tone (see p. 32) between its steps, and this is why the tune now sounds so strange.

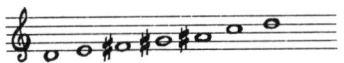

Whole-tone scale

In the new tone language that he evolved in these ways, Debussy composed piano pieces, songs, chamber music, one highly original opera, *Pelléas and Mélisande,* and several pieces for orchestra. The first of these, *L'Après-midi d'un faune,* created a sensation in the musical world, and it has retained its' freshness and magic to this day. Here is an extract from this work, just before the end:

Debussy: L'Après-midi d'un faune *(The Afternoon of a Faun, an ancient mythical god)*

Another French composer of outstanding originality was Ravel, who expressed his originality in quite a different way. In his music, as in that of Mozart and Chopin, we find the perfect balance between form and expression. His melody and harmony are original without losing sight of classical tonality:

Very slow

Ravel: Oiseaux Tristes *("Sad Birds")*

Fairly slow

Ravel (1875-1937): No. 2 of Valses Nobles et Sentimentales

His rhythmic patterns are clear-cut without being conventional:

Moderato

Ravel: Trio

In his orchestration, though he exploits the resources of the modern orchestra to the utmost, Ravel does this not for the sake of brilliant Impressionistic colour effects, but chiefly so as to make the line of the music clear. *Bolero* is an obvious example of this, because, though it consists of more or less the same tune played over and over again, Ravel's orchestration makes it so exciting that you hardly dare to breathe until it is over.

Both Debussy and Ravel wrote music for and about children. Debussy wrote a set of charming piano pieces called *Children's Corner.* Ravel's *Mother Goose* suite, originally written for piano duet, is often heard in the orchestral version which he later made of it. (It is delightful to play as a duet, and sounds much more difficult than it is.)

Moderato

Ravel: Mother Goose Suite - Little Tom Thumb, *lost in the forest*

Opera played a great part in the music of the Romantic era. In Italy, early in the century, Rossini, Donizetti, and Bellini had set a fashion that was copied all over Europe. Their music was very melodious, and decorated with lavish ornaments. Though difficult to sing, it was easy to listen to, and it was very good for showing off the vocal virtuosity of the brilliant Italian singers. Decorated vocal melody found its way into instrumental music and is a basic element of the pianistic style of Chopin and others.

Close on the heels of the earlier Italian opera composers comes Verdi, who gave the world some of its greatest operas. He was less interested than the others in providing singers with lavish opportunities for vocal display; his great desire—and his special gift, which he cultivated supremely in the course of his long and prolific career— was to find an exact musical expression for the particular dramatic situation. Add to this his unfailing flow of attractive melody, and it is small wonder that going to one of his operas is such a memorable experience.

Verdi (1813-1901): Prelude to Aïda

Verdi was copied by many other Italian composers, and though none of them could ever compare with him, some of them did produce operas that also have a permanent place in the operatic repertoire. The most popular of these include Mascagni's *Cavalleria Rusticana* and Leoncavallo's *Pagliacci,* two short operas usually performed together.

Another Italian composer much loved by opera-goers is Puccini, creator of *La Bohème, Tosca, Madame Butterfly.* Most of his opera plots deal with very dramatic subjects in a realistic manner. Puccini exploited their dramatic situations to the full with his gifts of touching melody and telling orchestration. In France many fine operas were composed all through the nineteenth century, from Meyerbeer and Halévy to Gounod and Saint-Saëns. Undoubtedly the most deservedly popular of these operas is *Carmen,* by Bizet, who also wrote

several other operas, some colourful incidental music to a play, *L'Arlésienne,* a symphony (when he was only seventeen), and an orchestral suite, *Children's Games,* originally for piano duet. The nineteenth century was the heyday of the *operetta* (light opera). The finest composers of this kind of entertainment were Offenbach and Delibes in France, Sullivan in England, Lehar and Johann Strauss in Austria.

Music for dancing goes on as an unbroken background throughout the Romantic era. Gone were the formal court dances of the seventeenth and eighteenth centuries; in their place the swaying waltz whirled its way through all the ballrooms of Europe. Foremost among the myriad composers of waltzes (apart from the Classical masters, from Haydn to Brahms, who all wrote delightful waltzes) are the members of the Viennese Strauss family, father, sons and grandsons all vying with one another in producing

Johann Strauss (1825-1899): Tales from the Vienna Woods

100

dozens and dozens of melodious compositions in this popular form.

Meanwhile, in the theatres, ballet was becoming increasingly important. The style was based on the fixed tradition of the seventeenth and eighteenth centuries, and the music written for it was similarly conventional and artificial, usually in the set forms of dances like the polka, the galop, the waltz, etc.

The ballet as we know it today is largely a product of Russia. Based on the traditional movements of Classical ballet, as imported from Italy and France, the Russian ballet infused new life into a dying tradition by adding the vigorous and expressive elements of Russian peasant dances. Besides this, new meaning was brought to the ballet by the expressive music written for it by Tchaikovsky. From a mere conventional entertainment or an expected interlude in every opera, the ballet came to have a life, a meaning and a character of its own.

The outstanding name in the history of the Russian ballet is Diaghileff, the great impresario (or manager). He was a meeting-point for all the arts, and he started off some far-reaching artistic activities. He had a unique mind, with an equal understanding of dancing, music and painting, as well as the genius to assemble them in a unity, so that each art could draw inspiration from the others. Thanks to his incentive, some of the leading composers of his day wrote some of their most successful music: Ravel his *Daphnis and Chloe,* Stravinsky his *Firebird* and *Petroushka.* Diaghileff also made a ballet out of Debussy's *L'Après-midi d'un faune.*

Owing to his far-reaching influence, Diaghileff may well be regarded as a turning-point in the history of music. All his composers were looking towards the future. And as their future is our today, perhaps it is time to look about us and see what is going on in music now.

LISTEN TO SOME OF THESE RECORDS

Schumann: Carnaval. *Chopin: Preludes, Mazurkas, etc. Mendelssohn:* Overture, The Hebrides; *incidental music to* A Midsummer Night's Dream. *Liszt:* Piano Concerto in E flat. *Berlioz:* Symphonie Fantastique. *Brahms: Symphonies, Concertos, Lieder, etc. Franck:* Variations Symphoniques; Sonata for Violin and Piano, *Dvorak: Symphonies,* Slavonic Dances, *etc. Grieg:* Piano Concerto; Peer Gynt Suite. *Tchaikovsky: Symphonies, Ballet music, etc. Borodin:* Polovtsian Dances *from* Prince Igor. *Rachmaninoff:* Piano Concerto No. 2 in C minor. *Sibelius:* Tapiola. *Wolf:* In dem Schatten meiner Locken. *Elgar:* Violin Concerto *(played by Menuhin). Delius:* On Hearing the First Cuckoo in Spring. *Debussy: Piano music, etc. Ravel:* Bolero, Daphnis and Chloe, *etc. Rossini:* Barber of Seville (Largo al factotum). *Verdi:* Aida; Falstaff; *etc. Bizet:* Carmen; Jeux d'Enfants - Suite. *And any other works mentioned in this chapter.*

CHAPTER TEN

Music Today

MODERN MUSIC · THE NATIONALIST TRADITION ·
REACTIONARY STYLES · NEW WAYS OF COMPOSING ·
ELECTRONIC MUSIC · COMPOSERS OF TODAY

IN MODERN LIFE, blue-prints take the place of day-dreams. Personal feelings are forgotten because scientific facts are so exciting. What were yesterday dreamed of as miraculous jet planes can today carry hundreds of passengers from breakfast in London to lunch in New York, and today's fantasies of interplanetary flight are the reality of tomorrow.

What the motor is in the world of travel, the microphone is in the world of sound, because it, too, telescopes time and space and opens up unlimited prospects. Thanks largely to this modern magic of the microphone, you can listen to a gramophone record today of a performance that took place a year ago; and on the radio you can listen in to a concert that is going on hundreds of miles away. Thanks also to the invention of the microphone, the tape-recorder has opened up an entirely new region in the world of sound. Strange new sound-effects whisper or whine, hiss or hiccough, shriek or blare at us, either as a background to some space-fiction film, or else as an independent composition in the field of electronic music.

How is music keeping pace with these staggering developments? As always, music is reflecting the life of the times. Some composers have found new ways of saying old things; others are using familiar means with which to say something new; others, again, have launched out into entirely new regions. The music-lover of today may well feel bewildered by all these different kinds of modern music. Hardly has he got used to one strange musical language than he is faced with some other music that sounds even stranger.

However strange and new it may seem, the new music is bound to have tempo and dynamics. Listen. Is it fast or slow, soft or loud? And does this help the music to convey a mood or feeling? If so, what?

If you hear some music that is so strange that you can't make head or tail of it, the thing to do is to listen hard for one familiar feature. What are the first things we noticed about music at the beginning of this book? First of all, rhythm. All right; listen for the pulses in the strange new music and start tapping—soon you may find that you can even beat time to it. But you will have to be on your toes, because one of the typical things in modern music is its frequent changes of bar time.

Now pitch. Whatever it is, the strange new music will almost certainly have definite pitch of some kind. Notice how it goes up and down, just as more familiar music does. The difference may perhaps be due to the use of a strange scale. Look at this tune. Have you ever heard it?

It is only the *Bluebells of Scotland* in the scale of C major, but with a sharpened fifth and a flattened second and seventh, like this:

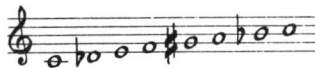

Here is a tune (by Bartók) in a strange scale. Play it several times as it is; and then reduce it to C major by ignoring the flats and sharps, and notice how different it sounds.

Béla Bartók (1881-1945): Mikrokosmos
Book II

Some composers write in more than one key at a time. Look at this tune:

Just a simple chord tune. Now look at this one:

Another simple chord tune, very like the first, which is made out of a C major triad, only this is made out of a G flat major triad, in a different position. But put them together, and there's a startling effect for you!

Brass instruments can be muted by placing a pear-shaped object into the open end to soften or change the quality of the sound

This is what Stravinsky did in his ballet music, *Petroushka,* and this is his entirely new theme, made out of an old-fashioned chord tune. Music like this, which is in more than one key at a time, is called *polytonal.* (Or *bitonal,* if it is in only two keys.)

Some music is in no key at all; the notes used are arranged in such a way that there is no home note. This kind of music is called *atonal* music. You can find examples of this on pp. 112/3.

Rhythmic patterns and phrases may not be easy to hear at first in modern music, but if you listen carefully you will certainly find them. You might even find, to your great surprise, that the phrases are comfortably balanced in pairs, like much of the music that you know. But more likely the rhythmic patterns are constantly changing, and this makes the phrases difficult to follow. In that case, listen for cadences. All music has to breathe somewhere, and once you can spot the cadences you are well on the way to getting some idea of the shape of the music. Here are some typical cadences in modern music:

Bartók: Divertimento for String Orchestra, *2nd movement*

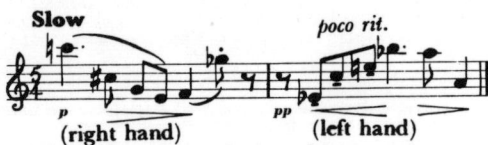

Elisabeth Lutyens: Piano e Forte *(Op. 43)*

Alan Bush: Men of Blackmoor: *End of the Opera*

Hindemith: Third Sonata *for piano, 1st movement*

Vaughan Williams: Sixth *Symphony, 1st movement*

Aaron Copland: Piano Sonata, *2nd movement*

If you are listening to a piece of orchestral or chamber music, there is the added interest of timbre. However difficult or confusing the music may seem at first, you can always get to grips with it by picking out one instrument, or group of instruments, and trying to follow what it is doing.

Now listen to some of the records listed at the end of this chapter. It is best to listen to a little at a time, and to the same piece often. Try to listen for the various things described above.

However strange and different it may seem, the new music is deeply rooted in the old. A number of features of modern music can be found in composers of the Romantic era.

Like Liszt and Wagner, and like Debussy and Scriabin, some modern composers have been making experiments in search of a new tone language. Other composers have felt, as all the national composers of the nineteenth century did, that the music of a nation, like its language, should express its own special character. As a Frenchman speaks French, so should he write French music; and as an Englishman speaks English, so should he write English music; and the same in other countries.

Towards the end of the nineteenth century there was a group of musicians in England, headed by Cecil Sharp, who felt that the natural musical speech of their people, as it could be found in genuine English folk-songs, was of very great value. They delved into the songs and dances of the countryside and hauled up priceless treasures. Among these musicians were two outstanding composers, Vaughan Williams and Holst, who absorbed the newly discovered folk-tunes so completely that they became the basis of their musical language. Here are some tunes from their compositions:

Vaughan Williams: Overture, The Wasps

Ralph Vaughan Williams (1872-1958)

Holst (1874-1934): "Jupiter" *from* The Planets

Apart from English folk-music, Holst had a wide variety of interests, ranging from the music of India and Africa to the music of the spheres! His orchestral suite, *The Planets,* is one of his best-known works.

Vaughan Williams, one of the greatest composers England has ever produced, is regarded as the "grand old man" of modern English music. He wrote nine symphonies, several of which have become classics of modern music. He also wrote many other beautiful works, choral and orchestral, vocal and instrumental.

Andante

mf He that is down need fear no fall,

He that is low, no pride. He that is humble

ev-er shall have God to be his guide.

Vaughan Williams: Pilgrim's Song from
Pilgrim's Progress

Others composers with a definitely English style are Arnold Bax and John Ireland. Their music sounds English not so much because they use English tunes (Bax used many Irish ones), but rather because they express themselves in ways which are typical of the English character. Their music has poetry, reticence and humour, and they do not go out of their way to make original effects.

In Spain, composers based their music on the colourful tunes and lively rhythms of their national songs and dances. Albeniz and Granados wrote chiefly piano music, while Falla

wrote some magnificent ballet music, including *The Three-cornered Hat*.

Moderato

This is the rhythm of the Miller's Dance

Moderato
Oboe

And this is the melody. This ornament is called a mordent, *and the notes in the bracket show how it should be played*

In America there have been many composers whose music has a definitely national character. Villa-Lobos uses Brazilian and other South American folk-tunes in his compositions, which are colourful additions to the modern orchestral repertoire. Ernest Bloch expressed Jewish religious feeling in his *Baal Shem* for violin and piano, *Shelomo* for cello and orchestra, and the *Sacred Service* for baritone, chorus and orchestra. George Gershwin wrote his music in the jazz idiom (which grew out of Negro folk-music of North America)—for instance, *Rhapsody in Blue* and the well-known folk opera, *Porgy and Bess*. Some American composers, for instance, Aaron Copland, have

The Miller's Dance from The Three-cornered Hat *by Manuel de Falla (1876-1946)*

Ballet from West Side Story, *a modern version of the story of* Romeo and Juliet, *with music by Leonard Bernstein*

investigated the music of the Red Indians and used certain elements of it in their compositions.

Hungary produced the two most outstanding composers of national music in Central Europe at this time. Kodály and Bartók both believed that there was something more in Hungarian folk-music than the popular gipsy music that generally passed for "Hungarian", and which was largely a product of the cities. They spent many years getting to know the true folk-music of the Hungarian peasants and their near neighbours, and their music is stamped with its character. But though they started out from the same point, the music of Kodály is entirely different from that of Bartók. We could think of Kodály as the bard or minstrel of Hungary; his music always speaks or sings, and much of it is in rhapsodic style; it tells of the joys and sorrows of the Hungarian people—in their everyday lives as well as in their history and legends.

Bartók, on the other hand, is a master-builder. Like those of earlier masters, Bartók's works are superbly organised, balanced and polished to the last detail. His music is fascinating to follow, partly because you can never be sure what he is going to do next. Like Beethoven, Bartók creates a new language for every one of his compositions, each one growing and developing in its unique way out of the musical seed that started it off (Example 1).

A further fascination is imparted to Bartók's music by the freshness and originality of his musical material, for as well as using Hungarian folk-tunes he sometimes uses the exotic scales and rhythms of Roumanian, Bulgarian and Turkish folk music (2 and 3).

Much of Bartók's music is difficult —both to play and to listen to. But

BARTÓK: CONCERTO FOR ORCHESTRA

1. *1st movement*

2. *4th movement*

3. *2nd movement*

4. *4th movement*

5. *2nd movement*

If you play the last example on the piano, holding the last chord on with the pedal, you can then tap the side-drum's rhythm on the lid of the keyboard

108

you need not be put off even by his most difficult works, for instance, the six string quartets. At the very first hearing there is always something—usually a tune—which you can grasp, and from then on you can perceive more and more of the quality of his music.

Fortunately Bartók also wrote a good deal of music that is easy to play, and some of it is very rewarding, such as the *Children's Pieces* for the piano, some of the duos for two violins, and some of the pieces in the *Mikrokosmos.*

Another great name in modern music is Hindemith. His compositions cover a vast range. He has composed easy pieces for young pianists and others for young string players; he has also composed sonatas for every instrument in the modern orchestra. All this by the way. In addition, he has written chamber and orchestral music of all kinds, operas (including *The Harmony of the World,* which contains his idea of music of the spheres), ballets, songs, piano and organ music. Last but not least, he has written some important books giving his own ideas about harmony and composition.

When he first started composing, Hindemith wrote more or less atonal music. But being one of the most practical musicians who ever lived, and wanting to provide music for beginners as well as for professional musicians, he soon decided that music, in order to make sense for the ordinary person, could not afford to ignore the natural laws of sound. Like Pythagoras in ancient Greece, he went back to the stretched string, as it were, and based his theories on the relationship of overtones to their fundamental tone. According to him, their order of importance is as follows:

Hindemith: Series I

Thus Hindemith restored basic tonality into his music, in a special and easily recognisable way of his own, as you may see from a typical cadence on p. 104.

Together with his new ideas about tonality, Hindemith uses every contrapuntal device known in musical history. For instance, look at these two extracts:

Hindemith: Beginning of Ludus Tonalis

Ending of the same work

They are the beginning and ending of a set of piano pieces called *Ludus Tonalis* (a game with tones), including twelve highly original fugues. Turn page 109 upside down and look at these two examples again. Do you see that they look the same as before? This is because for the second one Hindemith both inverted and reversed his theme—that is to say, he wrote it upside-down and backwards! But notice, in the second extract, how he makes sure we shall understand what the basic tonality is, by adding a straightforward C major chord at the end.

A number of fine composers have followed in Hindemith's footsteps: in England chiefly Franz Reizenstein and Arnold Cooke, and there are many more in other countries. Together with Hindemith, all these composers seem to have continued along the road first trodden by the great classical masters and further pursued in the Romantic century by Brahms, Bruckner and Reger.

Paris at the beginning of the present century was the centre of a fashion for exotic music. This was cultivated by all Diaghileff's composers, chief among them Stravinsky. One of the works he wrote for Diaghileff was music for a ballet called *The Rite of Spring*. It was a set of primitive ritual dances with exotic melodies, daring harmonies (chords full of "wrong" notes), fantastic rhythms and unheard-of orchestral effects. When it was first performed in a concert hall it was received with boos and catcalls. Today it ranks as a classic of modern music.

In the early nineteen-twenties a number of Parisian composers created a new fashion. Romantic feeling in music was out. Impressionism was out. National elements were out. Sonata form was out—or at least vastly modified. Witty entertainment was the order of the day, and parody

The Concert of Angels, *part of an altar-piece by Mathias Grünwald (early sixteenth century) which appears in the opera based on the story of this artist's life, called* Mathis der Mahler *(Mathias the painter) by Paul Hindemith, (1895-1963)*

reigned supreme. The best-known composers of this type are Poulenc, Milhaud, Satie and Prokofieff.

Stravinsky, who was also in Paris at that time, took the new attitude to extreme lengths and proclaimed that music has no meaning but itself. In other words, he denied that music can convey moods and express feelings, and concentrated entirely on the outer aspect of music—its forms, patterns and colours.

Tempo giusto

Stravinsky: Beginning of Dumbarton Oaks *Concerto for chamber orchestra*

Con moto

From the last movement of the same work

Stravinsky's style of composition at this period was utterly different from the vivid music of his early ballets, and was in the style known as *neo-classical*. This meant partly a return to eighteenth-century conditions of music-making, such as Classical tonality, contrapuntal style and small combinations of voices and instruments. But neo-classical could also mean an attempt to recapture the Classical spirit of ancient Greece, as is suggested by Stravinsky's use of ancient Greek legend and drama in *Oedipus Rex, Persephone* and other works.

Meanwhile, in Vienna, the city of Mozart and Beethoven, Schubert and Brahms, the old musical ideals were being juggled with in a different fashion. At the beginning of his career, Schoenberg tried to express himself in what was almost a copy of Wagner's style. He soon came to a dead end and decided to strike out on a new road in music. His first work in revolutionary style was called *Pierrot Lunaire* (Moonstruck Pierrot). It was a setting of some delightfully crazy

111

poems by a French poet, Giraud. Just as Lewis Carroll used the crazy "Alice" stories in order to break down accepted ideas of space and time, so Schoenberg used the crazy "Pierrot" poems in order to break down accepted ideas of melody, harmony and rhythm. In this work the singer had to half sing, half speak the lines. Here is a passage about Pierrot when he is half collapsing with terror, because he thinks that the moon looks like a polished scimitar just coming down to cut his sinful head off.

Fairly fast

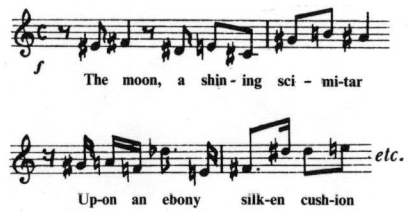

Schoenberg (1874-1951): Pierrot Lunaire

Can you find the home note in this? Actually it is C sharp, but the tonality of this music is so vague that it is practically lost; in other words, it is very nearly what we would call atonal music.

After writing *Pierrot Lunaire* and some other works in similar style, Schoenberg invented a method of composing which he called *twelve-tone technique.* Taking the twelve notes of the chromatic scale as his basis (see p. 32), he decided that the whole of a piece of music must be made out of what he called a *tone-row.* Here is an

example of a tone-row, from his *Suite for Piano,* Op. 25.

As you see from this, a tone-row contains all the notes of the chromatic scale, and none of them comes in more than once.

The thing that mattered in the tone-row was the order in which the notes came. Once he had fixed this, the composer was free to sound his tone-row upside-down or backwards, or both upside-down and backwards, and even some or all of the notes together. In his *Piano Suite,* Schoenberg divided his tone-row into three parts. In the Gavotte he started off with part one in the right hand and part three in the left hand.

Rather slow

In the melody of the Minuet he used part two.

Moderato

(The E flat is repeated only to help the crescendo.)

Besides Schoenberg himself, the outstanding composers of twelve-note

112

music in the early part of this century were Berg and Webern. Berg wrote some music that is very lyrical, in spite of its strange idiom. He contrived to graft the new methods on to some of the old, and to unify them by his own individual genius; for instance, his *Violin Concerto* incorporates a Bach chorale. His best-known opera, *Wozzeck,* a sad tale about a simple soldier, ends with a scene where children are playing. Here is part of their song:

Alban Berg (1885-1935): Wozzeck

Webern's music opens up a new world again. You might call him a musical prophet of the Atomic Age, for he was a poet of the infinitesimal. He created a tone language so fine, so subtle and so concentrated, that it demands an entirely new kind of musical intelligence from both performers and listeners. Most of his works are very short, usually lasting only a minute or two. Here, in strange disguise, are melody and harmony, imitation and variation, tension and climax. As you can see a world reflected in a drop of water, so you can perceive a world of music in these crystals of sound.

Anton von Webern (1883-1945): Variations for Piano *Op. 27 (The numbers show how the same chords are used in the second half as in the first, but in reverse order)*

Schoenberg's method of composing has taken music along widely different paths. Not all modern composers want to abandon tonality, but some of them think it is a good idea to invent a special set of rules for each of their compositions. They have even gone beyond making rules about the order of notes in a tone-row, and they now make rules for relating pitch to durations, durations to degrees of dynamics, and so on. They call this "serial technique", and they talk of "serialising" pitch, or "serialising" pitch and durations, etc. They say that it doesn't matter what rules you make, so long as you apply them throughout the piece.

Does all this seem terribly complicated? Actually it is quite easy to do. For instance, you could decide that you will write a piece using the notes of a certain scale, say C major, with the pitch of the notes related to the pulses in a certain way, like this:

113

Crotchet (one pulse) related to one scale step (interval of a second) = C to D, or D to E, etc. Minim (two pulses) related to two scale steps (interval of a third) = C to E, or D to F, etc. Dotted minim (three pulses) related to three scale steps (interval of a fourth) = C to F, or D to G, etc. Semibreve (four pulses) related to four scale steps (interval of a fifth) = C to G, or D to A, etc. and so on. Then you could try to write a fragment of tune bearing this in mind something like this:

Having made a bit of tune, you could balance it by another.

These two short phrases could be balanced by one longer one.

How do you like it?

Quite a harmless, ordinary-sounding tune, you might say. Now, supposing you used, instead of a major scale, a chromatic scale. This is what the piece would sound like:

Don't you like it? Well, perhaps it is rather gloomy. Then make up a scale, any kind you like, or, if you can't think of one yourself, use the one on p. 103, then transfer the tune to it and see if you like it better.

A little piano piece could be made out of the same tune (but in half time), something like this: it could start in C major and modulate to the dominant; the middle section could start on C with a drone bass; then the same thing transposed to F; then a recapitulation of the first tune, slightly altered to go with the drone bass.

114

This little experiment is just to show you that even when a composer is using quite an artificial order in his arrangement of notes, making them into music depends on a number of things which have never changed since music began: mood—expressed in tempo, dynamics and phrasing; balance of phrases; repetition, variation and contrast; tension and climax —that is, the growth of each phrase towards its cadence, and of all the phrases towards the final cadence; arrangement of sounds in pitch, that is, tonality (or even bitonality, polytonality or atonality); and order of sounds in time—that is, rhythm.

★   ★   ★

Some composers of today have gone so far in serial technique that they seem to have left music behind. Or you might say they have swung full circle and are now back in the realm of Nature music. For instance, Messiaen, the French composer, writes music that is based on the notes and rhythms of bird-song.

Allegro

Messiaen: Réveil des Oiseaux (*Awakening of the birds) for piano and orchestra - Thrush*

Especially does this seem to be so in the field of electronic music, for here the materials of music sound as if they come from sounds in Nature, like rippling, bubbling and rushing water, bird-calls and animal noises, to say nothing of rumbles and claps of thunder. And, indeed, some of these sounds do come from Nature, for electronic music can be divided into two categories; pure electronic music, in which the sounds are made by sound generators, and *musique concrète* (or concrete music), in which the sounds are made by natural means.

On the one hand, composers of *musique concrète* create their musical material by recording actual sounds, such as bird-calls, on a tape-recorder. They then distort these sounds by playing them at different speeds to change their pitch, or by playing them backwards to get various strange effects. They might record the sound of someone tapping on a milk-jug, and change its pitch by re-recording this sound and playing it at different speeds; then they could join all the various lengths of tape together and produce a tune, all made out of one tap on a milk-jug! Or they might analyse sounds like breaking glass or china by recording them on tape and then playing them back slowly. And after that they proceed to compose music out of these sounds. Or perhaps they might cut off the basic tones and use only the overtones, or put the whole sound into an echo-chamber and then cut off the echo and use only that.

On the other hand, composers of pure electronic music have been experimenting with sounds produced by electronic sound generators. They call the different kinds of sounds by the names of colours: for instance, "white" noise contains all the overtones (which means, of course, that there is no level of pitch not sounding, just as white light contains all the colours of the spectrum). The effect is a very harsh sound, rather like steam escaping from a railway engine. "Pink" noise is made by filtering "white" noise—that is, by taking out some of its overtones.

Some composers use a combination of all these techniques—both pure electronic music and concrete music —in their compositions. A famous example is the *Gesang der Jünglinge* (Song of the Youths), by the German composer, Stockhausen. It consists of the sound of a boy's voice and pure electronic tones treated with serial technique (see p. 113). The words are also "serialised", and so are even some syllables of the words.

Another new departure in modern composition is indeterminate music, where some aspect of the piece is left to the choice of the performer. In this kind of music, the performers have a number of different passages to play, and are then let loose, so to speak, to play them in almost any order, so long as they all finish up together. The pioneer of this kind of music is John Cage, an American composer who has also written a work, called *Imaginary Landscape,* for a strange collection of instruments, including an electric oscillator, tin cans and electric buzzers.

Naturally, some composers of today are interested in all these and other possibilities. But there is something that most of them realise, and that we should bear in mind too, and that is: what matters most is not where the composer gets his sounds from, but what he does with them.

Especially is this true of so-called *avant-garde* composers. Hearing them for the first time, you might well think they are purposely trying to get right away from music as you know it. These young composers, following the lead of famous experimenters like

Composers of electronic music, have had to invent new kinds of notation. Here is a specimen from No. 2 of Electronic Studies *by the German composer Stockhausen. As you see, it looks more like a graph than a musical score, because it all had to be worked out mathematically. The sounds are built up of pure tones from an electronic sound generator*

Stockhausen or Boulez, Ligeti or Berio, come up with strange mixtures of tunes and improvisations (like jazz), tonality or atonality, live music and electronic sounds. Sometimes it seems to make sense, sometimes it seems like nonsense. But it is always worth giving these daring young composers a fair try. For in all these experiments there might just be the one composer who can open for you a magical gateway to new and strange spheres of musical adventure.

Here are a very few of the leading composers of today: in America, Samuel Barber has written some splendid music for orchestra; Aaron Copland and Elliott Carter have both created individual styles by their original approach to rhythm; in Soviet Russia, Prokofieff and Shostakovitch have written music in cosmopolitan style; in Italy, Dallapiccola, while using twelve-tone technique, nevertheless contrives to produce music that has a truly Italian melodious quality.

In France, Messiaen and Boulez, both experts in serial technique, are attracting a number of young composers to Paris. In Holland, Badings, whose earlier style was similar to that of Hindemith, is now experimenting with electronic music. In Germany the best-known modern composers, apart from composers of electronic music, are Blacher and Henze.

In England there is a galaxy of com-

Picasso's The Three Musicians *(in the Museum of Modern Art, New York)*

posers, some of whom were once thought very daring indeed, such as Arthur Bliss, Master of the Queen's Music, William Walton, composer of a truly great First Symphony, Michael Tippett, Elisabeth Lutyens and many others.

One could say of Benjamin Britten, as was once said of Schubert, that he "could set even a poster to music". This special gift of being able to say everything in musical speech that is immediately understandable, is obvious in all Britten's numerous compositions, from his simple—but most ingenious—settings of folk-songs, to the operas that have made him world-famous, such as *Peter Grimes* and *The Turn of the Screw*; also in a later masterpiece, the *War Requiem* and his recent opera, *Death in Venice*. Much of Britten's music is written with children in

117

Benjamin Britten, born 1913

Britten: "Fisherman's Round" *from*
Peter Grimes
(*Tremolo *see Index*)

mind: *Let's Make an Opera, Young Person's Guide to the Orchestra,* the exquisite *Mass* for boys' voices, *Noye's Fludde,* and many others.

Many British composers of today had their first hearing in the open rehearsals, concerts and workshops of the Society for the Promotion of New Music. They compose in a great variety of styles, from the almost traditional to the outrageously experimental. A few of many available names are Malcolm Arnold, Richard Rodney Bennett, Harrison Birtwistle, Alun Hoddinott, Gordon Crosse, Peter Maxwell Davies, John Gardner, Alexander Goehr, Nicola LeFanu, Jonathan Lloyd, Elizabeth Maconchy, Nicholas Maw, Bernard Rands and Hugh Wood.

Try to hear records or broadcasts of music by these and other modern composers. When you find something which attracts you, listen to it often.

LISTEN TO SOME· OF THESE RECORDS

Vaughan Williams: Job; Tallis Fantasia; *Symphonies, etc. Holst:* The Planets; *etc. Bax:* Tintagel - Symphonic Poem. *Ireland: Songs and piano pieces. Falla:* The Three-cornered Hat. *Bloch:* Baal Shem *for violin and piano; chamber music, etc. Gershwin:* Porgy and Bess. *Samuel Barber:* Adagio for Strings. *Aaron Copland:* Billy the Kid - Ballet Suite. *Kodály:* Hary Janos. *Bartók:* Concerto for Orchestra. *Hindemith:* Concert Music for Brass and String Orchestra. *Stravinsky:* Firebird; Petroushka: Rite of Spring. *Schoenberg:* Pierrot Lunaire. *Berg:* Violin Concerto. *Webern:* Five pieces for Orchestra. *Britten:* Spring Symphony; Missa Brevis in D. *Tippett:* Four Ritual Dances. *Walton:* First Symphony; Belshazzar's Feast. *And any other works mentioned in this chapter.*

118

CHAPTER ELEVEN

Musical Occasions

PERFORMERS · OPERA AND CONCERT-GOING · SINGING,
PLAYING AND COMPOSING

THE CONCERT world offers a wide choice of musical treats. If you go to an orchestral concert you will enjoy it much more if you get to know some of the music before you go. Never fear that it might lessen your enjoyment of, say, a Beethoven symphony if you listen to it even dozens of times on the radio or on records before you hear it at a concert. A live performance can always throw new light on a great work, however well you know it. Besides, there is the added fascination of watching the orchestra and knowing what to expect from the various players.

If you go to a piano recital, or hear a famous pianist play a concerto with orchestra, you might think, "What a wonderful life, to be a concert pianist!" But the life of a concert pianist is not easy. You might think that, once a musician has learnt a work, he knows it for ever. Not at all. There is no end to the new discoveries a true artist can make about a work, even if he has known and performed it all his life.

On this page is Clifford Curzon comparing several different editions—and taking advantage of the sunshine in his garden at the same time.

Not only must the concert pianist keep a great deal of music in his head, but he must keep his fingers supple too. Some pianists do part of their

daily practice on a dumb piano (a small keyboard not connected to any strings), so that they can exercise their fingers without tiring their ears. In this way they can keep their ears fresh for the music. In the first of the three pictures on this page, Clifford Curzon is just about to begin. In the next picture he is in deep concentration working at the piano, where he spends many hours each day — that is, when he is not away on his concert tours. And finally you can see him sharing the delightful fruits of his talents and labours with the spellbound audience at a "Prom" concert. Notice how conductor and soloist manage to keep contact even though the piano is placed in front of the orchestra, as it usually is for a piano concerto.

At the age of eight, the young violinist opposite played a full programme of some of the most difficult music in the violin repertoire—in masterly fashion. Can you guess who he is? The answer is in the lower picture.

Ever since the wonderful Italians of the eighteenth century, there has been an unbroken dynasty of great violinists, such as Paganini, Joachim, Kreisler, Heifetz and many others. Some have carried their audiences away by the sheer virtuosity of their playing. Others have been musicians first and foremost, and have moved their hearers by their deeply felt interpretations of great music. Menuhin is

Allegro

A quotation from Elgar's Violin Concerto *(1st movement), in which Yehudi Menuhin (below) often performs the solo part with great distinction*

Pablo Casals (1876-1973)

man of wide sympathies. His performance of Bartók's *Violin Concerto* so impressed the composer that he wrote a work especially for him — the *Sonata for Unaccompanied Violin.*

Casals was the supreme re-creator of great music. Not only cellists, but conductors, violinists, pianists, in fact most musicians, look up to Casals in such a way that they could well say, as Haydn did of Handel, "He is the master of us all." Casals spent all his life pursuing a simple ideal: the faithful re-creation of the composer's thought. He said that the heart of the matter is in the shape of the music, and that you can enter into and express all the meaning of the music by "re-discovering its live shapes".

Bach: Suite No. 2 in D minor *for unaccompanied cello*

of this class. When he was only twelve, his performance of the Beethoven and Brahms concertos had an inspired quality that made it unforgettable. Listeners felt that he really knew what the composer meant, and that he was able to communicate it fully and truthfully. His playing did not say, "Can you hear how well I play?"; it said, "Listen to this marvellous music!"

This extraordinary boy grew into a

Playing string quartets — and listening to them — is one of the most absorbing and fascinating pursuits in music. In Vienna people meet in each other's homes at least once a week for regular quartet playing. Some years ago, three Viennese students, Norbert Brainin and Sigmund Nissel, violins, and Peter Schidlof, viola, enlisted an English fellow-student, Martin Lovett, cello, for regular quartet playing. After a time they began giving concerts,

122

The Amadeus String Quartet   *Janet Baker as* Dido   *Dietrich Fischer-Dieskau*
(*see page 39*)

and since then, under the name of the Amadeus Quartet, they have gone from strength to strength. But though they are now international celebrities, the intimate quality of their playing has remained unchanged.

Great singers are rare, and great Lieder singers rarer still. Dietrich Fischer-Dieskau and Janet Baker both have lovely voices, both are superb musicians, both are wonderful interpreters, both are equally happy — and equally impressive — on the opera stage and on the concert platform. Listening to a song recital by either artist is a haunting experience.

Opera at Glyndebourne, a small opera house in the country (Sussex), where operas are performed in ideal conditions every summer. The picture shows the final scene in Verdi's Falstaff: "Windsor Forest by Moonlight" at the end of which all the characters turn to the audience and sing, "All the world's a comedy". Verdi made this into a brilliant fugue, which begins like this:

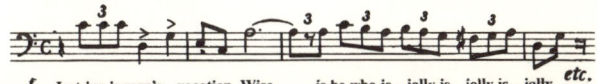

Should you join an orchestra, you might even perhaps be given the chance some day, like Lance Hartland (the boy in this picture seen talking to the world-famous conductor Andre Previn), to try your hand at conducting

If you have an opportunity to go to the opera, it is a good idea to find out all you can about the story. In many operas the dramatic action seems confused, partly because it is often difficult to hear the words (which may be sung in a foreign language anyway), and it is a great help to know what it is all about. You will then be free to enjoy the music and to notice how it expresses, colours and emphasises the dramatic action. So — get hold of the libretto (the text of the opera) and learn it by heart! Or if not by heart, at least read it through once. Or better, twice.

Since singing is so good a thing,
I wish all men would learn to sing.

William Byrd said this nearly five hundred years ago — and he might have said it today. Nothing can quite take the place of making music yourself, whether it is singing, playing or composing. As you get to know a work from the inside, by singing or playing it, so the music comes to life in your mind more and more.

If you like singing you can join a group or a choir. Most schools have choirs, and these sometimes take part in big public performances, like the one you can see in the frontispiece.

Music comes alive for you in a special way if you play an instrument, particularly if you play chamber music or if you join an orchestra. If you play in a school orchestra, you might, in time, be able to join one of the National Youth Orchestras. These meet for study courses, in various parts of the country, and they usually end with a public concert.

Should you be a budding composer, and if you have friends who play or sing, why not persuade them to try out something of yours? Imagine the thrill of hearing a composition of your own being performed for the first time — even if it makes you want to rewrite every note!

Remember, music is always beginning.

124

Index and Glossary

Diatonic, notes used in major or minor scale
Diminution, 48
Discord, jarring combination of sounds, 16
Divisions, variations, 37
Dominant, 5th note of major or minor scale 15, 32
DONIZETTI, Gaetano (1797–1848), 99
Double, (to) using same notes but higher or lower
Double bar, 28
Drone, continuous note of fixed pitch, 24
Duet, (or Duo) a piece for two performers
DUKAS, Paul (1865–1935), 9
DUNSTABLE, John (c. 1370–1453), 36
DVOŘÁK, Antonín (1841–1904), 94
Dynamics, levels of loudness or softness, 8
Electronic music, 115
ELGAR, Edward (1857–1934), 96
Enharmonic, change of name but not of pitch, 73
Ensemble, (on-*som*-bl) a group of performers
Episode, contrasting section in fugue or rondo
Exposition, full statement of main themes, 48, 62
FALLA, Manuel de (1876–1946), 106
FARNABY, Giles (c. 1560–1640), 37
FAURÉ, Gabriel (1845–1924), 94
Figured bass, figures indicating basic chords, 44
Finale, (fee-nah-lay) ending-piece, 44
Fine, (fee-nay) end, 44
First inversion, triad with middle note as bass
Flattened, half a tone lower
Folk-songs, traditional songs, 23
"Forty-eight, The" 47, 48
FRANCK, César (1822–1890), 93
Frequency, rate of musical vibrations, 17
FRESCOBALDI, Girolamo (1583–1643), 49
FROBERGER, Johann (1617–1667), 49
Fugal, in the style of a fugue
Fugue, a style of contrapuntal composition, 48
Fundamental, root note of series of overtones, 18
GARDNER, John, (b. 1917), 118
Gavotte, dance in $\frac{4}{4}$ time starting on 3rd beat, 42
Generator, machine for making electronic sounds, 116
GIBBONS, Orlando (1583–1625), 37
Glissando, sliding from one note to another, 85
GOEHR, Alexander (b. 1932), 118
GOUNOD, Charles (1818–1893), 100
Great Staff, 25
GRIEG, Edvard (1843–1907), 94
Ground, bass tune repeated through a piece, 39
GUIDO D'AREZZO, (c. 990–1050), 25
HALÉVY, Jacques (1779–1862), 100
HANDEL, George Frideric (1685–1759), 41
Harmonics, overtones, 18
Harmony, the art of combining chords, 15

Harpsichord, keyboard instrument, 41–2
HAYDN, Joseph (1732–1809), 63
Heckelphone, a type of bass oboe, 86
HENZE, Hans Werner (b. 1926), 116
HINDEMITH, Paul (1895–1963), 109
HODDINOTT, Alun (b. 1929), 118
HOLST, Gustav (1874–1934), 105
HUMFREY, Pelham (1647–1674), 38
Imitation, copying a tune in another voice, 47
Impresario, organiser of artistic ventures, 101
Impressionist, a style in painting and music, 97
Improvisation, playing and composing at once, 23
Incidental music, music written to be played before, during or between parts of a play, 39
Instrumental music, music for playing
Interlude, short piece of instrumental music between two parts of a vocal or instrumental work
Interpretation, how a performer presents what he feels the composer wants, 120
Interval, distance in pitch between 2 notes, 16
Inversion, a tune upside down, 48
Jazz, popular American dance-music, 106, 117
Key, (a) a lever operated by fingers
         (b) major or minor scale of a piece
Key signature, sharps or flats on each line of music, indicating its key, 32
KODÁLY, Zoltán (1882–1962), 107
LASSUS, Roland de (1530–1594), 36
Ledger lines, extra lines above or below the staff for very high or very low notes, 32
LeFANU, Nicola (b. 1947), 118
LEONCAVALLO, Ruggero (1858–1919), 100
Libretto, the book of words of an opera, 124
Lied, (leed) a German romantic song, 73
LIGETI, György (b. 1923), 117
LISZT, Franz (1811–1886), 91
LLOYD, Jonathan (b. 1948), 118
LULLY, Jean-Baptiste (1632–1687), 41
Lute, early stringed instrument (like guitar)
LUTYENS, Elisabeth (b. 1906), 117
MACONCHY, Elizabeth (b. 1907), 118
Madrigals, part-songs for several voices, 36
MAHLER, Gustav (1860–1911), 96
Major, scale or chord with bright effect, 14
Manuscript, music written by hand, 30
Mass, musical setting of a church service, 46
MASCAGNI, Pietro, (1863–1945), 100
MAW, Nicholas (b. 1935), 118
Mazurka, Polish national dance in $\frac{3}{4}$ time, 94
Mediant, 3rd degree of major or minor scale, 15
Melody, a tune shaped like a song, 15
MENDELSSOHN, Felix (1809–1847), 90

126

127